D0115863

Association of National Advertisers

DAGMAR:

Defining Advertising Goals for Measured Advertising Results

Second Edition

Solomon Dutka

First Edition by Russell Colley

♺
Printed on recyclable paper

ANA
Association of National Advertisers, Inc.

NTC Business Books
a division of *NTC Publishing Group* • Lincolnwood, Illinois USA

Library of Congress Cataloging-in-Publication Data

Dutka, Solomon
    DAGMAR : defining advertising goals for measured advertising
results / by Solomon Dutka ; original edition by Russell Colley.
        p.   cm.
    Includes bibliographical references (p.   ).
    ISBN 0-8442-3422-2
    1. Advertising.   2. Advertising—Evaluation.   I. Colley, Russell.
II. Title
HF5823.D84   1995
659.1'1—dc20   94-41435
                                                                                    CIP

Published in conjunction with the Association of National Advertisers, Inc., 155
East 44th Street, New York, New York 10017.

Published by NTC Business Books, a division of NTC Publishing Group
4255 West Touhy Avenue
Lincolnwood (Chicago), Illinois 60646-1975, U.S.A.
© 1995 by NTC Publishing Group.
Manufactured in the United States of America.

5 6 7 8 9 BC 9 8 7 6 5 4 3 2 1

Contents

Part One
The Power of an Objective   1

Part Two
How to Go About the Job of Defining Advertising Goals   21

Part Three
The Meaning of Measured Advertising Results   41

Part Four
Advertising's Purpose in Your Business   57

Part Five
Brief Examples Illustrating the Definition of Advertising Goals   89

Example/Product

Exhibits

Foreword

There's no subject in the advertising and marketing process which has been as discussed, debated, criticized, or sought after as the measurement of advertising effectiveness.

While many measurement techniques, methodologies and theories have appeared on this topic over the years, few have stood the test of time. *Defining Advertising Goals for Measured Advertising Results* (DAGMAR) has stood this test for over thirty turbulent business years. DAGMAR is a true classic of business literature. It has educated generations of advertisers on how to think about and how to evaluate their advertising expenditures.

It was a labor of respect, recognition and affection when the A.N.A. Advertising and Marketing Research Committee undertook the project to update DAGMAR.

One of the ongoing tenets of A.N.A. is the enhancement of the science of advertising and marketing for the benefit of both industry and consumers. DAGMAR is an ongoing vehicle in support of this objective.

We're deeply appreciative of the efforts of Sol Dutka and his associate, Lester Frankel of the firm of Audits & Surveys who authored this update of DAGMAR.

They captured its original thrust while keeping it current, complete, and correct.

Special thanks go to a team of volunteers who agreed to help guide the author and then shared the task of reviewing and commenting on the draft:

Shelly Newman, Pfizer Incorporated, New York, NY
Francine Ross-Berger, Combe Incorporated, White Plains, NY

Thanks also go to Matt Miller, Renée Paley, and Phil Shyposh of the A.N.A. Staff for their efforts in bringing forth this revision.

Ernest J. Fackelman
Chairman
A.N.A. Advertising and Marketing
Research Committee.
Vice President, Business Information
and Analysis
R.J. Reynolds Tobacco Company
Winston Salem, North Carolina.

About the Author

Solomon Dutka, Ph.D., is Chief Executive Officer of Audits & Surveys, Inc. He is also an Adjunct Professor of Statistics at New York State University's Graduate School of Business Administration.

Prior to founding Audits & Surveys in 1953, Mr. Dutka was Chief Statistician for both Dun & Bradstreet and Elmo Roper Associates.

For his work in nuclear physics on the Manhattan Project during World War II, he was awarded a citation from the Secretary of War. He served as an American Statistical Associate Delegate to the United Nations Sub-Commission on Statistical Sampling and as a member of the United States Census Advisory Committee.

Mr. Dutka is a Fellow of the American Statistical Association and of the American Association for the Advancement of Science. He is a past President of the Market Research Council, which presented him with its 1984 Hall of Fame Award "in recognition of contributions of outstanding and lasting value to the practice of market research."

He serves on the Board of Governors of Daytop Village, a narcotics treatment center, is a member of the World Business Council and the Chief Executives Organization; as a member of the Board of Trustees of the Neurosciences Institute served on the Advisory Board of the United States Information Agency (USIA) Private Sector Market Research Committee; and, for six years was a member of the United States Census Advisory Committee.

Mr. Dutka began his professional career as a statistics instructor at Columbia University's Graduate School of Business Administration. He has written numerous articles and books on statistical techniques and their application to marketing and marketing research. His books include *Sample Designs for Marketing Intelligence Surveys* and *Notes on Statistical Sampling for Surveys*, plus *How to Conduct Surveys* and *A Dictionary for Marketing Research*, which he co-authored.

Advertising & Marketing Research Committee

Ernest J. Fackelman, *Chairman* R. J. Reynolds Tobacco Company
Mario Abate Warner-Lambert Company
John Almash MasterCard International
Charles Battista Frito-Lay, Inc.
Lori Bush Amoco Oil Company
Carleton R. Crowell 3M Company
Paul DeVries Stouffer Foods Company
Joan Flesch Chesebrough-Pond's, USA
Jonathan Kalan Oral-B Laboratories
Michael A. Kelne Southwestern Bell Telephone Company
Ron Levitt Citibank
Sara Lipson Shearson Lehman Brothers
Thornton C. Lockwood AT&T
Susan Morganstern Bell Atlantic
Dennis Q. Murphy Hewlett-Packard
Richard A. Nelson Campbell Soup Company
Sheldon Newman Pfizer Incorporated
Andrew Pasheluk Lorillard Tobacco Co., Inc.
Jerry Payne Coca-Cola USA
Francine Ross-Berger Combe Incorporated
Holly Ryerson Bristol-Myers Squibb Company
Patricia Schlaugies CPC/Best Foods
Dannis Shirley SmithKline Beecham Consumer Brands
David A. Simler Digital Equipment Corporation
Pamela South Schering-Plough HealthCare Products
Richard Tongberg Brown-Forman Corporation
Wendy Ward Thomas J. Lipton Co.
Mary Wells Du Pont Company

Introduction

In 1961, the Association of National Advertisers published *Defining Advertising Goals for Measured Advertising Results* (known in the trade as DAGMAR). This publication demonstrated how attaining advertising objectives can be greatly enhanced through (1) the use of clearly defined advertising goal-setting procedures and (2) ongoing measurements of their achievement.

Over the years, the DAGMAR concept has proven both popular and useful to advertisers, agencies, media researchers, and universities. Because of continuing demand, this publication has seen eight subsequent printings, the last in 1984. This revision, written in 1992, keeps to the same principles originally presented, updating them as needed and adding new insights generated from their continued application.

During this past 30 years, advertising expenditures in the United States have increased tenfold from $12 billion to $130 billion, spurring many changes in the marketing environment in which today's advertising operates. Retail marketing trends have given rise to increases in convenience stores, fast-food outlets, warehouse clubs, factory outlets, catalog sales outlets, and channel marketing, to name a few changes. Direct marketing has increased, as well. Consumer and dealer promotions have burgeoned. Indeed, for many companies, such promotional budgets exceed dollars spent on more conventional advertising. In-store advertising and point-of-sale promotions have likewise increased, as has a more recent growth area, event marketing. The consistent advertising and promotion of industrial products are no longer a rarity, nor are Global Marketing and Global Advertising viewed merely as interesting academic concepts.

Furthermore, new feedback measurement techniques at the store level have evolved, such as Universal Product Code scanners at the cash register. Companies can now better assess their retail advertising and marketing efforts even daily, should they desire. Through the use of computer-assisted telephone interviewing (CATI), fast feedback on consumer attitudes and behavior as well as other critical aspects of marketing intelligence are obtainable.

New technologies have also enabled marketers to improve the quality and reliability of their products. The Deming Prize for quality control in Japan and the Malcolm E. Baldridge National Quality Awards in this country are manifestations of the universal recognition associated with quality improvement. To their credit, in an era of technology, companies are also increasingly aware of the customer service and satisfaction component in a consumer's perception of their product. Advertising and promotion are now being employed, not only to sell products, but to build a sound relationship between the consumer and the producer.

Despite these changes, the question addressed by DAGMAR, as well as the concepts that were introduced, are as relevant today as they were in the 1960s. The use of these DAGMAR concepts during the past 30 years has enabled marketers to further improve the effectiveness and the dollar efficiencies of their advertising communication. It has proven to be both a process and a discipline. Also, this revision benefits from the experience gained in the use of DAGMAR by our company and other research organizations, and by those advertising and agency marketing research departments that measure the extent to which specific advertising goals are achieved as a fundamental part of their marketing efforts. Examples of these have been updated to reflect more current products and practices.

This revision also affords us the opportunity to clarify questions about DAGMAR and its implementation which have arisen since its publication.

It is our sincere hope that new and former readers continue to be absorbed by the vitality of this concept as well as profit from its use.

Part One
The Power of an Objective

The history of business teaches us the power of advertising in bringing together buyer and seller. The history of all human endeavor—military, religious, political, and industrial—teaches us the power of a well-chosen objective.

Here we explore:

Advertising by objective . . .
The result may well add exponential growth to advertising's power.

1. Advertising Results Can Be Measured

Almost everyone closely associated with advertising has a deep-rooted interest in measuring advertising results. Advertisers, who are the final decision-makers and who pay the bills, want to know what return they are getting on their advertising investment. Advertising agencies need to demonstrate to advertisers that they can and do produce effective advertising. The very existence of an advertising medium depends upon convincing both agency and advertiser of its ability to deliver results.

In recent years, the combined talents and resources of advertisers, agencies and media have made substantial progress—through research—in solving many problems related to advertising. These research efforts suggest that a solution to the ultimate problem of measuring overall results of advertising may be within reach.

In the years since World War II, expenditures on advertising in this country have increased more than 33-fold. They trebled from 1945 to 1961 and then, along with the growth of television, increased 11-fold from 1961 to 1992. This dramatic growth rate is, in itself, evidence of business's sustained belief in advertising's economic efficacy. To American business, advertising is an increasingly integral force in competitive selling, in introducing new products coming out of the laboratory and in establishing brand equity and corporate identity.

Advertising is a force that increases the productivity of a company's communications efforts. It will deliver a sales message for pennies (or a fraction of a penny)—compared with dimes to deliver a selling message via retail salespeople and dollars per selling message delivered via the manufacturer's sales staff. Advertising's share of the sales dollar is on a rising curve because it has increasingly become a more efficient means of marketing communication than these others. Business people know this. But a general belief, faith and confidence in the overall power of advertising is insufficient to substantiate the realities of a corporation's ongoing advertising expenditures. Most companies continuously face such questions as:

- *How much should the company spend on advertising?*
- *How much should be spent on product A versus product B versus overall corporate advertising?*
- *Should the company decrease, maintain, or increase its expenditure level?*
- *How should the company make "buy," "switch" or "hold" decisions on major media and copy themes?*

It would be a mistake to assume that the A.N.A. has discovered any easy answers to these difficult questions. No single formula, however complex, can provide for their solution. What is presented, instead, is a proven approach that leads consistently to better answers to these questions. This approach, briefly stated, is as follows:

- *It is virtually impossible to measure the results of advertising—unless and until the specific results sought by advertising have been defined.*

  Conversely:
- *Advertising results can be measured IF specific advertising goals are first defined.*

Like many solutions to difficult problems, the approach may seem both simple and obvious—especially to those who expected that a solution would be in the form of a revolutionary research technique. To emphasize, this approach is not a new *research* technique, but, rather, a *management* technique. Simply, it is the application of the principle of *management-by-objective* to the field of advertising:

> It starts with the simple statement that to measure the accomplishment of advertising, a company must first have a clear understanding of the specific results it seeks to accomplish through advertising. ∎

2. Distinguishing Advertising from Marketing Objectives

Since the ultimate purpose of the advertising and marketing of consumer products and services is to induce purchasing, the distinction between advertising and marketing objectives often remains unclear. Advertising, which is only a part of marketing, is concerned with producing psychological effects such as "brand preference." Marketing, on the other hand, covers all functions—including advertising—which are part of the process of moving goods (or services) from where they are manufactured or assembled to the consumer or user. Mr. Woodruff, president of the Coca-Cola Company, set the stage for the phenomenal growth of Coca-Cola when he defined its marketing objective in 1931 as maintaining "Coca-Cola within arm's reach of desire." This prescient marketing philosophy is a unique and, by now, classic example of combining the behavioral components of marketing with the psychological effects of advertising.

The question, "What are your advertising objectives?" has been asked and will continue to be asked of the thousands of people who create or approve advertising. Most companies have a ready answer to the question. However, closer examination frequently shows that their answers express broad corporate or marketing objectives rather than the specific goals of the advertising.

Indeed, certain crucial questions often remain unanswered:

1. How many companies present their overall *corporate* objectives in written measurable terms?
2. How many have a set of specifically defined *marketing* objectives?
3. Is it reasonable, or possible, for companies to expect to arrive at concrete advertising objectives unless their marketing objectives have been thought through and agreed upon?

It can be illuminating to look at a company's latest advertising plan. Chances are, it is labeled something like "Advertising Plan (or Budget), ABC Company, for the year." In a large company, there may be such a document for each division or product group. The "Advertising Objectives" section (if such a section is included) probably contains phrases like:

- *to increase sales*
- *to expand share of market*
- *to aid the sales staff in opening new accounts.*

These statements are broad generalities. It becomes impossible to measure progress if objectives are stated in such general terms. More specific objectives may be stated, such as:

- *to increase sales by 10% in year . . .*
- *to expand share of market from 10% to 12% over the course of the year.*

These, too, are problematic because they are *total marketing* goals, not *advertising* goals. Obviously, advertising cannot accomplish the objectives alone. A company must be much more specific if it wants to measure the *particular* contribution advertising makes to its total marketing effort. Thus, the first job is to define specifically what a company expects to accomplish through its use of advertising.

3. Advertising Goals Defined and Illustrated

An advertising goal[1] is a specific communication task, to be accomplished among a defined audience to a given degree over a designated period of time. ■

Here we have a definition. It conveys fuller meaning when we take it apart, examine each piece carefully, and illustrate the entire advertising process with examples.

Let's examine two examples, one a consumer product, one an industrial product, which illustrate advertising goals. (Additional examples, covering many different types of products and industries, are provided in Part Five.)

Example 1: Laundry Detergent

The product is a brand of laundry detergent (the example is fictitious but typical). Let's assume that the marketing goal is to increase share of market from 10% to 15% in three years.

Advertising is one important force in achieving this goal. However, advertising does not and cannot perform the job singlehandedly. Distribution is important. So are packaging, point-of-sale display, and price. And, of course, attaining the marketing goal depends, in the final analysis, on the product itself—whether it provides sufficiently desirable consumer benefits.

Specifically, then, what part of the total marketing goal do we expect advertising to perform?

The answer to that question is the key to realistic, measurable advertising goals. Advertising should not be assigned tasks that it is incapable of fulfilling. Advertising is a *communication* force. As such, it should be assigned a communication task. Its job is to deliver a sales message—not just to *expose* a message to people but to *deliver* a sales message that stimulates or ultimately leads to behavior.

What sales message do we want advertising to deliver? Here we must be specific:

- *Do we want to convey the message that Brand "X" with new ingredient "Y" is a low-sudsing detergent which cleans clothes better and faster than other brands?*

- *Do we want to convey the message that Brand "X" saves costly repair bills and messy suds spillover?*

Our job, at the goal-defining stage, is not to write copy. We are not concerned with *how* to say it, but simply with *what* needs to be said.

Let's assume that, based upon other research, we arrive at the following goal:

> To increase—from 10% to 40% in one year—among the 70 million homemakers who use automatic washers, the number who identify Brand "X" with ingredient "Y" as a low-sudsing detergent which cleans clothes better and faster than others. ∎

We now have a specific communication task that can be performed by advertising, independent of other marketing forces. It thus becomes feasible to measure advertising accomplishment. As a matter of fact, as we continue to gain goal-setting and goal-accomplishment experience, we can better answer the ever-present advertising budget enigma, "How much advertising is required?" Of course, before setting our goal, we conducted research to find out how many people already had the message we wanted to deliver. For example:

	Before Advertising Campaign	After Advertising Campaign
Message registration	10%	40%

The research indicates that the message has gotten through to an additional 30%. Companies will often pre-test the whole process in test markets before a national introduction. Now we have a basis of decision-making to look at such questions as:

- *How many more* users *do we have among those who can play back the message?*
- *Are we acquiring new users (and retaining old ones) at an affordable rate?*

- *Should expenditures be increased and the process speeded up?*
- *Can expenditures be decreased?*

With defined goals and measured results we have a basis to evaluate both copy and media. Using test markets, for example, we can analyze questions like:

- *Does copy approach "A" get the message through to more people than copy approach "B"?*
- *Does medium "C" do a better job at lower cost than medium "D"?*

Consumer package goods manufacturers are accustomed to conducting research into consumer buying habits and advertising penetration. Clearly, translating such marketing intelligence into specific advertising goals improves the efficacy of the resulting advertising.

Example 2: Drilling Bit for Oil Wells

This example illustrates the use of defined advertising goals for an industrial product, a drill bit used to drill oil wells. The bit is made of a special steel alloy that increases its life, on average, by 25%. The cost of a drill bit, while considerable, is a small percentage of the total cost of drilling a well. The time required to drill the hole is the key factor, since contractors generally charge by the foot or hour. The big appeal, then, is the savings in overall drilling time and costs. Such savings can be demonstrated by engineering tests.

The market consists of oil companies who do their own drilling, contractors who drill the wells, and distributors who sell bits and other supplies. The total number of "buying influencers" is estimated at 15,000, including engineers, superintendents, and other technical and managerial personnel who participate and have an important voice in the specification and purchase of drill bits.

Research shows that only 50% of the 15,000 buying influencers are acquainted with the new, superior drill bit. And only 25% of those people are familiar with the claim that this bit reduces net overall drilling costs.

Each of the company's 10 salespeople makes an average of 20 sales calls per week and each sales call costs the company an average of $290. It would take the sales force 1½ years to make just one *informative* sales call on each of the 15,000 buying influencers. It is obviously much too expensive in money and time to use salespeople to convey the intended message:

1. *That this product exists*
2. *That it offers decided cost reduction advantages.*

Advertising's job is to deliver prospects who are both aware of the product and who understand its advantages, while the salesperson's job is to convince those prospects that the product can be applied to their particular technical problems, to get buying action, and to aid customers in successful product application.

The Advertising Goal

The advertising goals for this hypothetical product might then be:

- *To raise the number of buying influencers who are acquainted with the product from 50% to 75% in the next year*
- *To increase the number who get the message— "reduces overall drilling cost"—from 25% to 50% in the next year.*

Separating advertising's tasks from the total marketing job to be done allows us to focus creative effort on carrying out an identified task. Now we can measure more accurately how effectively advertising performs its assigned role.

4. Why Not Use Sales Results as a Yardstick of Advertising Performance?

When asked the purpose of advertising, most people would say, "That's easy—the purpose of advertising is to sell goods." So why do we bother to define advertising objectives over and above the obvious aim of making a sale? Specifically, why isn't advertising performance measured in terms of sales results alone?

It certainly would be convenient if we could tote up sales results at the end of the month or year and use them as a yardstick of advertising effectiveness. Recent developments in measurement methodology (such as the retrieval of warehouse withdrawal data as well as computerized check-out records at the retail level) have made current sales data easily and quickly accessible. The availability of such precise information has encouraged the view that sales provide the best measure of advertising productivity. Even if this were feasible, experienced advertising and marketing executives know that it is dangerous to assume that if sales go up or down, advertising deserves the credit or blame. There are compelling reasons why it is misleading for both advertiser and agency to assume a direct causal relationship between advertising and sales.

First, consider the function of advertising and its definition:

> Advertising is mass communication, directed to consumers, the ultimate purpose of which is to impart information, develop positive attitudes, and aid in inducing action beneficial to the advertiser (generally, the sale of a product or service). ∎

Alfred Politz, a pioneer in the application of scientific methodology to marketing research, pointed out that while "purchase is the ultimate purpose of advertising, purchase behavior per se is a strictly physical activity. The effects of advertising, on the other hand, are psychological phenomena."

Many variables intercede between an advertising-induced positive disposition on the part of a consumer to buy a product (which advertising may have helped induce) and its actual purchase. Let us examine some of them.

First, there is a set of variables over which the advertiser has no control. For instance, an ever-changing economic climate affects sales. Demographic changes, no less so. Political events (such as the 1991 Gulf War or elections) keep people glued to their TV sets, thus altering their buying and leisure patterns. As every soft-goods retailer knows, both weather and seasonality have their effect. The sales patterns of many products and services such as cold remedies, outdoor home equipment, vacation travel cruises, skiing equipment, and insecticides reflect different seasonal effects. Nor do our competitors remain static. They keep improving their products, their styling, their distribution, their prices, and their advertising and promotion, sometimes as a consequence of, or independently of, what we have done in our advertising.

Finally, it is important to distinguish between discretionary and nondiscretionary choice in the purchase of a brand. At a sports arena, for example, a spectator, through advertising, may be committed to a certain brand of beer, Brand A. But if he is thirsty, and only Brand B is available, he will purchase that one. The executive who has to take a certain flight to meet a customer in another city at a specific time may be obliged to take other than his favorite airline. Here, advertising has little to do with the customer's selection and purchase of Brand B.

Advertising is only one of the many forces that must be blended to aid in consummating a sale. By acting in unison with other complimentary forces at the disposal of the advertiser's marketing, promotion, and sales departments, a marked effect on sales can result. How these operate is shown in the vector diagram. (See Exhibit A.)

Exhibit A   Vector Diagram

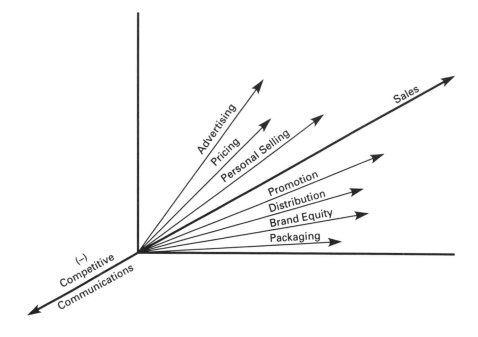

The vector diagram is used by engineers and physicists to measure the resultant of many forces applied to a system. Marketing is essentially such a system. The lines within the diagram are called vectors. A vector is any quantity which has direction and magnitude. The larger the magnitude of these marketing forces and the smaller the angles between the vectors—the more they pull together—the greater will be their effect on the resultant—the sales of the product.

Let us examine the advertising vector in this relationship. The advertising for some marketing situations may represent a few pennies of the marketing dollar. Conversely, it may be the dominant marketing force. But unless advertising is the dominant marketing force (outweighing all of the other marketing forces combined, including the impact of competitive efforts, distribution, and a changing marketing environment), it is difficult to establish a direct positive relationship between volume of advertising and volume of sales.

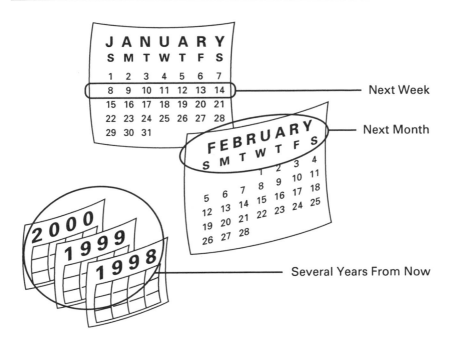

In essence, current sales figures are not the final yard-stick of advertising performance unless one or more of these factors are present:

1. *Advertising is the single variable.*
2. *Advertising is the dominant force in the marketing mix.*
3. *The proposition calls for immediate payout (such as in mail order or retail advertising).*
4. *There is no change in the marketing environment.*

These conditions seldom prevail among so-called "nationally advertised" products. Consequently, analysts who take an accounting-financial viewpoint (defining advertising productivity as the ratio of the marginal sales dollars returned by advertising investment to the total dollars invested to produce and place the advertising) may understate or overstate the true value of the advertising effort but not know it.

As already pointed out, the broader purpose of advertising is not necessarily limited to the production of direct sales. Its impact can be manifested in other ways. Advertising can lead to inquiries (especially in the case of industrial products), automobile showroom traffic and test drives, the use of the Yellow Pages, or discussions with friends. It also provides background for retail promotions. For nationally and internationally distributed products, advertising creates, supports, and enhances "brand equity"[2] in the minds of customers.

Part of the confusion surrounding the measurement of the impact of advertising and defining relevant and productive advertising goals is the lack of distinction between the terms *advertising effects, advertising effectiveness,* and *advertising efficiency.* Let us clarify the terms, all of which are amenable to ongoing measurement when used as part of advertising goal statements:

- *Advertising effects:* Absolute measures of advertising effects on such variables as awareness, knowledge of brand's properties, and attitudes toward brand.
- *Advertising effectiveness:* Relative measure of change in advertising effects.
- *Advertising efficiency:* Is there a more economical way to achieve the same levels of advertising effects or effectiveness?

In summary, advertising is only one of the many critical forces that must be blended in order to consummate a sale.

5. Put It in Writing

"Why define our objectives?" some may ask. "It's obvious what we are aiming to do. Everybody connected with advertising in our company and agency knows this. So why go to all the bother of writing it down?" To those who feel this way, the following experiment cannot help but have some value:

Ask several people in your agency who are most closely concerned with your account to write down their version of your advertising *objectives*. Now do the same among approval-level people in the advertiser organization. Include the marketing, sales and product managers, the chief financial executive, and, by all means, the chief corporate or operating executive.

Don't be surprised when you get back generalities that apply to the total marketing effort, not to advertising's unique role in marketing. Imagine the results had you asked the same question about the specific advertising goals.

Many people find it difficult to define specifically in writing what they expect advertising to accomplish. If you can draw them into a discussion of objectives, you may well find wide differences of opinion. The sales manager may look upon advertising as a means of selling extra carloads of goods next month, while the advertising manager may be concerned with building a brand franchise. The company president may look upon advertising as a force that builds the corporate name and reputation. And so the varied opinions will go, through all of the echelons of people who contribute in some way (in the copy, art, media, research efforts) to the making and the approval of advertising.

6. Principles

In outline form, the principles of the approach we recommend are:

1. Advertising goals are succinct statements of the *communication aspects* of the marketing job. (They express the particular work advertising is uniquely qualified to perform and do not encompass results that require a combination of several different marketing forces.)

2. The goals are expressed in writing—in finite, measurable terms. (If there is agreement among all of those concerned on what advertising is expected to accomplish, then it is no great chore to reduce it to writing. If there is lack of agreement as to purpose, the time to find this out and correct the problem is before the advertising is prepared, not afterward.)

3. Goals are agreed upon by those concerned at both creative and approval levels. (Thus, planning is separated from doing. Agreement is reached on *what needs to be said to whom* before time and money are spent on *how best to say it.*)

4. Goals are based upon an intimate knowledge of markets and buying motives, i.e., they use valid and statistically reliable marketing intelligence. They express realistic expectancy, not mere hopes and desires, in the light of carefully evaluated market opportunities.

5. Benchmarks are set up against which accomplishments can be measured. (For example, the product brand equity among consumers, including items such as product knowledge, image and attitudes, and buying propensity, are appraised before and after the advertising, and among those reached versus those not reached by the advertising.)

6. Methods to be used at a later date in evaluating accomplishments are determined when goals are established, not after the advertising is launched.

With this outline in mind, let us discuss and illustrate these principles in detail and answer some questions raised by this approach to advertising measurement.

7. What Are the Benefits?

Another question raised concerning the difficult problem of advertising measurement goes like this: Advertising has moved ahead. It continues to make its contributions to sales and profits—so why all this fuss about defining advertising goals?

We look for the answer by considering some of the benefits of defining advertising goals:

- **People do better work when they have a clear idea of what they are driving at.** History and psychology tell us this is true in all branches of human endeavor. Things get done better and faster when there is a common sense of purpose. Often, truth is so obvious that it is overlooked. The copywriter and the artist who, in the final analysis, create advertising, can beam in on the target with greater impact, and less wasted effort, if they are given a clear understanding of what that target is.

- **Advertising is perhaps the most intangible of all business forces.** It is particularly important to have clearly defined goals when dealing with an intangible force. Perhaps it is less essential to have well-defined goals in some of the most tangible areas of the business. The production department can see its accomplishment in terms of finished goods inventory. It has visual evidence of wasteful practice in terms of size of the scrap-loss pile. Not so for advertising. The sales force sees and talks to customers. They have a mental picture of customer reaction based on first-hand contacts in their territories. They can even re-enact sales scenes and conclude, "Why I made (or lost) the sale." Not so for advertising.

- **Goals have become more necessary because advertising has become more specialized.** Copywriters of yesterday did not have the help of researchers and other specialists. Relying on insight, they were on their own in developing themes. Advertising and marketing today represent the combined talents of a team of specialists whose contributions are enhanced when and if advertising objectives are clearly understood.

- **Agreed-upon goals reduce wasted effort.** How often do we go through a dozen roughs or semi-comprehensives only to discover that "This isn't what we want to say at all." This process of beating out objectives with art, typography, TV storyboards and film is like building a house without blueprints. A goal is simply a device for resolving differences of opinion, for getting minds together on what needs to be accomplished. A goal rivets people's attention to the important and the pertinent. Hence, it is a great labor-saving device. Furthermore, it enables managers, who have many products or campaigns under their supervision, to detect whether a particular ad or campaign has strayed off its intended course.

- **A goal avoids the waste that results from "compromise advertising" and indecision on the question: "What message do we want to convey to what audience?"** Such vague advertising is an attempt to consolidate the divergent objectives of various people on the *sending* end and thus communicates no strong central message to those on the *receiving* end—the customers.

- **Goals assist the creative team.** What a grave error it would be to misjudge a goal as a restrictive device on creativity! It is, in reality, a *protective* device for today's creative advertising people. It says to the advertising professional, "This is *what* we want to communicate; you are the expert on *how* best to communicate. Use all of your ingenuity to accomplish this specific communications task. We will judge your creative work by the results obtained, not by second-guessing."

- Finally, returning to the main thesis of this book, goals make possible the measurement of results. Measurement, of course, is not an end in itself. It is only a means to an end, which, here, is more productive, more profitable advertising.

The Necessity of Rules

Discipline allows creativity to flourish. The case for rules was elegantly stated by the painter Sir Joshua Reynolds in 1768. His words are quoted by Stephen Bayley in *Taste: The Secret Meaning of Things* (Pantheon):

> Every opportunity, therefore, should be taken to discountenance that false and vulgar opinion that rules are the fetters of genius. They are fetter only to men of no genius; as that armor, which upon the strong becomes an ornament and a defense, upon the weak and misshapen turns into a load and cripples the body which it was meant to protect. . . . How much liberty may be taken to break through those rules . . . may be an after consideration when the pupils become masters themselves. It is then, when their Genius had received its utmost improvement, that rules may possibly be dispensed with. But let us not destroy the scaffold until we have raised the building. ■

Notes

1. The terms "objective" and "goal" are often used interchangeably. For our purposes, the following distinction is made throughout the book:

    OBJECTIVE: A broad aim, desirable end. For example:

    Corporate objective—to make a profit
    Marketing objective—to sell goods
    Advertising objective—to create brand preference

    Objectives go on year after year with little or no change. We rarely achieve our objectives (either group or personal) in the sense of complete fulfillment (e.g., happiness, prosperity). To measure accomplishment it is necessary to become more specific.

GOAL: A goal is an objective that has been made specific as to time and degree of accomplishment.

Corporate goal—to earn 10% on invested capital in 199X
Marketing goal—to achieve 22% of total industry sales by 200X
Advertising goal—to establish a 20% preference for Brand "A" among X million housewives in 199X . . .

2. Brand Equity: The goodwill adhering to a brand name. It can be measured in dollars and cents. It is reflected in the price difference a consumer is willing to pay to obtain one brand rather than another.

Part Two

How to Go About the Job of Defining Advertising Goals

Where to start?
Who should define the goals?
What information is needed?
What are the pitfalls?

8. The First Step in Advertising Management

All managerial work, unlike Caesar's Gaul, is divided into four broad areas: planning, organizing, executing, and measuring. The first step in managing is to "define the objectives" and the final step is to "measure achievement of objectives." Here, then, are some common sense guidelines on how to go about the job of defining advertising goals.

Work Involved

Responsibility for getting the job done may rest with the company advertising director or manager, the agency, the director of marketing or sales, or the product managers. The job might be instigated by top management with parcels assigned to various persons. In any event, all of the above-named persons should at least participate. We will assume that the leader is the advertising director or manager, and that he or she has the full support and cooperation of top management, the agency, marketing, sales, and finance and research management.

If the scope of the task includes the entire product line, the advertising director would be well advised to break it down into segments (perhaps by product line or brand) and assign them to different people. The workload should be organized so that thinking and planning do not get pushed aside because of day-to-day operating details. The leader would do well to set a time schedule with interim check-points and will no doubt have frequent occasion during the project to recall the wisdom of Sir Joshua Reynolds: "There is no expedient to which a man will not resort in order to avoid the real labor of thinking."

Perhaps the best course of action is to concentrate first on a single area of the business, such as one product line, do a thorough job in this one area, and then use the process as a prototype for other segments of the business in the future.

Some Guidelines

The following guidelines bear repeating; they will help avoid many difficulties encountered by those who have attempted to define advertising goals in the past:

1. An advertising goal expresses results that can reasonably be expected from advertising (not results that require all of the combined forces of marketing).
2. The advertising goal is agreed upon by both advertiser and agency *before* the advertising campaign.
3. The goal is expressed in written, measurable terms.
4. There is a starting benchmark against which progress can be measured.
5. The goals are based on a reasoned analysis of opportunities after gathering the most complete, relevant, valid marketing intelligence available. (Again, they are not based on hunch, hope, or a mere extension of past performance.)

The pivotal concept is that advertising tasks must be separated out of the total marketing mix.

An advertising goal does not express results that require the combined forces of marketing. This subject was addressed briefly in Part 4. Here is a simple illustration.

Let's assume our product is a make of automobile. It would be unreasonable to set as an advertising goal:

| "To sell 1,000,000 cars next year." ■

The specific-year model design, when announced, may or may not be a "hit" with the public. The distribution organization may or may not be equipped to convert informed, interested, emotionally favorable prospects into customers. Competitive cars may be perceived as more preferable. The economic climate and the weather may enhance or inhibit the public's mood to buy. It is unreasonable and unrealistic to judge the performance of advertising *solely* on the basis of sales results. Advertising may do *its job* magnificently, yet be unable to counteract other factors beyond its domain.

A Definition of Advertising's Job

Here we have reached the heart of the problem. Precisely what is advertising's job in the total marketing scheme? This is where misconceptions and misunderstandings among various people involved often occur. The purpose of advertising is to perform certain parts of the communicating job with greater economy, speed, and coverage than can be accomplished through other means:

> Advertising's job purely and simply is to communicate, to a defined audience, information and a frame-of-mind that stimulates action. Advertising succeeds or fails depending on how well it communicates the desired information and attitudes to the right people at the right time and at the right cost. ■

There are perhaps a hundred different items of information and attitude regarding the product that should be considered, weighted, and sifted down to one or more major messages and the several subsidiary messages which may be considered. It is this sifting process, rather than the information-gathering process, with which we are primarily concerned.

Here again, we stress the need for the end product of the process (clearly defined and agreed-upon goals) to be in *writing*. If there is true understanding and agreement on the messages to be conveyed to a specific audience, it should be easy to reduce them to a written statement of the key messages (that is, *what* is to be said, not *how*).

9. Inside-Out and Outside-In Information

Despite the great quantities of statistical and descriptive data that most national advertisers have on products, markets, and media, the information in many instances has not been screened, weighed, interrelated, and boiled down to the terse statement of intended accomplishment we have stressed. When we consider this information in terms of our need to define advertising goals, we recognize two types, which we shall call "inside-out" information and "outside-in" information.

Inside-out information includes data about products and competitive products, industry sales history, trends and forecasts, distribution policies and channels, pricing history and practices, past advertising and promotion expenditures, themes, media, etc. Such information is necessary and valuable to advertising professionals. They should have access to it, study and digest it.

Many experienced people can gather this kind of information; it does not require the particular skills and imagination of advertising executives, whose great contribution is that, by training and intuition, they think in terms of the end customer (*outside-in* thinking). Their thinking runs like this:

- Merchandise: What is there about this product that would make *other people* want to buy it?
- Markets: How many of what types of *people* compose the present and potential markets?

- Motives: What desires, habits, and attitudes cause *people* to buy or refrain from buying?
- Messages: What outstanding things can we say about this product that will move *people* to buy it?

Advertising supplements the traditional contribution of those trained and oriented toward the inside-out point of view with the outside-in point of view.

In recent years, a number of companies have recognized the importance of strategic marketing and advertising planning. Some have done an extremely thorough job of gathering and cataloging product and marketing information in great detail. Some of this information consists of available statistical and product data—that is, inside-out information. Other segments of this information base deal with outside-in data on the habits, characteristics, attitudes, and motivations of *people* who comprise the market.

All of this information can be extremely valuable. But it is a misnomer to label such data a "plan." The data merely provide background information. The plan itself may be only 10 pages rather than 10 pounds of data. The essence of a plan is a goal, representing, in a single page or paragraph, the *decision* which has grown out of months or even years of research, thinking, and planning.

It states in a few words:

- *This is the message we want to deliver.*
- *This is the audience we want to reach.*
- *This is the degree of goal accomplishment we expect to achieve.*
- *This is the target date for goal achievement.*

10. Information Needed to Define Advertising Goals

The information-gathering process is nothing more than the *systematic* application of research, experience, and judgment to questions previously mentioned. These questions have been expanded into what we shall call the 6M approach to defining advertising goals:

- Merchandise: *What are all the important benefits of the products and services we have to sell?*
- Markets: *Who are the people we want to reach?*
- Motives: *Why do they buy or fail to buy?*
- Media: *How can they be reached?*
- Measurements: *How do we propose to measure accomplishment in getting the intended message across to the intended audience within the designated time frame?*
- Messages: *What are the key ideas, information, and attitudes we want to convey in order to move prospects closer to the ultimate aim of a sale?*

There is nothing new about the elements of this process. However, these elements continue to operate in an increasingly dynamic marketing communication system. Early advertising professionals had a much simpler product line to think about. Markets, consumption habits, distribution, and media were less complex. Fewer people were involved in the creation and approval of advertising. Competition was less keen. Today's product lines have become longer and more complex. Consumption habits and motivations, never static in the past, are no less so today. Many different people with a greater variety of professional backgrounds have become involved in the process of creating and approving advertising. In view of these changes, a systematic approach to the question, "What specific messages do we have to convey to what particular audience?" is called for.

Perhaps the only new aspect of this advertising goal approach lies in bringing the various pieces of information together into a succinct statement of what we aim to accomplish through advertising. Gathered information must be translated into strategy and that strategy must then be expressed in terms of specific goals. Measurement then becomes feasible.

We begin with a critical analysis of the information required to define goals. It would be useful to have a universal checklist applicable to every situation in every company and industry. But, of course, each company and product is different. Questions that apply to consumer goods do not necessarily apply to the industrial goods advertiser. Questions that apply to high-turnover, low cost-per-unit items (candy, soft drinks) may not apply to high-cost, low-turnover items (cars, major appliances, or homes).

The inevitable conclusion is that advertising directors who want to make a solid start in the direction of defined objectives and measured results will need to construct their own outline or checklist. In doing so, they will confine the checklist to only those questions of importance in their companies or for their products.

Below are some thought-starter questions.

Information About Merchandise

To define our advertising goals, what are all the things we need to know about the products and services we have to sell? For example:

- *What are all of the conceivable benefits (advantages, features, uses) of our product and services from the ultimate customer's point of view?*

- *Is there one benefit that stands out above the rest?*

- *Are there secondary or supplementary benefits that are important to certain segments of the market?*

- *What are the customer benefits beyond the product itself (packaging, availability, service, and reputation, etc.)?*
- *What are the benefits (advantages, etc.) of products directly or indirectly competitive?*

It would be helpful to have a complete and consolidated history of the product, its uses and advantages in relation to competition, with a detailed background of the market and competitive marketing and communication efforts over time. This perspective may also include the review of relevant analogies from other product categories. It is crucial to distill the product information down to the essence. Conclusions must be reached and decisions made on the key product features and product advantages from an advertising standpoint. *It is this distillation process that concerns us, not the mere collection of product information.*

11. Who Buys?

Here again, many advertisers have access to huge amounts of information about markets, such as statistical information available from company sales records, marketing research, and industry and government sources. For example:

- Industry past sales data (by product type, brand, year, season, geographic location, etc.)
- Forecasts of industry sales
- Competitive share-of-market estimates.

Such data are vitally important to advertising planning. In addition, these sources will also provide consumer-oriented data which will cover:

- The number of people who constitute the present and potential markets

- The complete gamut of relevant sociological and psychological information about these people needed to communicate with them in terms of their particular needs, desires, and interests, including:
- Their demographic characteristics (age, sex, geography, socio-economic group, etc.)
- Their consumption habits: incidence, frequency and quantity of use. The relative buying influence of various people (adults and children, husbands and wives, purchasing agents and engineers, etc.).

The concept often overlooked by those who have not been intimately associated with advertising is that markets are *people* with certain similarities or common denominators. The term "market" can conjure up a geographical mental image: the Cincinnati market, the San Francisco market. Markets may also be transitory as, for example, people who suffer from hay fever during certain periods of the year, the newly married, persons who take overseas trips, pregnant women, etc. Advertising thinking must be fully oriented to groups of people, wherever they may be, who have similarities in characteristics, habits, and interests: the teenage music market, the small-car market, the home-computer market, the business-copier market, the market for robotics in each of various industries, the market for jeans, or the athletic footwear market, to name but a few specific markets, each with unique advertising goals.

The outpouring of new products from research laboratories continues to grow. Many successful corporations have found that 50% or more of their sales come from products or industries that did not exist a decade ago. Additionally, new uses are being discovered for existing products. In 1992, for example, one-third of Johnson & Johnson's sales came from products introduced in the previous five years. (*Wall Street Journal*, 12/22/92, p. 11)

Advertising professionals must have an intimate understanding of the size and character of the market for each product. Further, they must see the total market in terms of its segments. Creative marketers/advertisers will often seek to exploit and expand such "niche" markets they have uncovered. Examples of such markets are diet soft drinks, all-natural toothpaste, decaffeinated coffee, fat-free ice cream, low-fat cheese products, and high-fiber cereal.

It is difficult to generalize about thousands of advertised products, which include consumer package goods, consumer durables, and industrial goods; hence, a few examples for discussion follow (figures are fictitious).

Our Product Is Coffee

We know that more than half of the population of 217,000,000 persons in the United States who are 8 years of age and older drink coffee at least once a day. However, U.S. coffee consumption is declining. To counter this trend, research has suggested marketing strategies which may be considered individually or in combination. These include (1) advertising the different types and blends of coffee on the market such as espresso, cappuccino, Turkish and mocha, (2) getting restaurants to feature these varieties in the beverage sections of their menus, (3) promoting coffee in cans and making it available in cans from vending machines.

Our Product Is Cereal

A key to advertising strategy may be reliable, up-to-date market information on how much is consumed by adults versus children, and child-adult influence on brand selection, as well as attitudes toward such factors as health, diet, sugar, and snacking. What is known about ways to convince adults that cereal is also an adult breakfast food?

Switch now, from consumer to industrial goods. Think of the necessary information if our product is high-strength steel used for pressure vessels, or computers used by banks for demand deposit accounting, or chemicals used in petroleum refining.

Advertisers need to ask, "What is the total size of our market in terms of people?" (Note that market size is not comprised of *companies*—companies do not buy industrial products; *people* within companies do.) Specifically, then, what is the composition of our market? Is it, for example:

- 6,100 purchasing agents in textile mills?
- 25,250 engineers in the aircraft industry?
- 44,000 officers of banks or insurance companies?

Such size and character-of-market figures need not be exact. Reasonable estimates will do. But a company should have some useful approximation of the size of the market in terms of people to whom messages will be directed. In one instance, an industrial market which was presumed to be limited to 50,000 company purchasing agents, was found to include nearly 500,000 individuals who had an influence on the buying decision. The latter, more accurate, figure was estimated after consideration was given to the *people* within companies rather than the number of companies to be reached.

Intimate background knowledge of the influence of each person connected with the buying decision on the final choice is taken for granted in personal selling. Salespeople who call on an industrial account know (or should know) the relative importance of various people who influence the purchase of their products. They know what is of particular interest to the project engineer, the superintendent, and the purchasing agent. They may often be accompanied by a technical salesperson as well. And, if they are good at sales, they design their sales presentation according to the interests of particular prospects. They allocate their selling time according to the influence their prospects have in consummating a sale. Marketing research carried on nationally and further analyzed by Standard Industrial Classification Code can be of invaluable assistance in preparing such presentations.

12. Why Do They Buy?

Many honest and competent researchers in independent research companies, advertising agencies, and corporate research staffs can provide reasonably reliable answers to the questions:

- *Why do people buy or fail to buy our product?*
- *What are the rational and emotional attitudes of prospective users toward our product, toward our company?*
- *Why do people buy our competitor's products?*
- *What are the unmet needs in the product category?*

Researchers are able and willing to put their experience, knowledge, and skill to work for you. It is the advertising manager's job to think through and spell out, with the clarification of information gained by research, the answers to the question:

- *What do I need to know about the motives, attitudes, habits, and characteristics of the people to whom I will address advertising messages?*

Again, without attempting to compile an exhaustive checklist, let's examine a few critical areas of inquiry.

Buying Habits and Characteristics

Certainly we should find out as much as possible about the buying habits and demography of the people who comprise the potential market for our product. We want this information broken down by those who buy our brands and competitive products, plus potential users who may not presently use the product type. We will certainly want these data graded out by "regular" and "occasional" users—for example, among gasoline buyers, the steady customers of each brand and the "switchers." For many retail establishments, such as roadside service stations, purchases by occasional buyers may exceed those made by regular buyers. Here, location or convenience may be more critical to purchasing than brand preference: generally, for consumer goods, we will want a complete rundown on characteristics, such as sex, age, socioeconomic status, geographic location, and consumption habits of present brand users, users of competitive products, and potential users. In industrial goods, we will want to know the industry, the application, the position or title of individuals, and their relative influence in industrial goods specification, as well as new industrial products the company is working on in its research and development area.

We will certainly want our prospects graded on the basis of their quantity of consumption: thus, the man who buys a case of beer a week consumes 17 times as much beer as the man who buys one 6-pack a month. A confirmed tea-drinking family uses a lot more tea than one that merely keeps tea on hand to serve guests.

Answering these questions is, of course, conventional practice.

Buying Motives and Influences

"Why do people buy?"

- *Is it some physical aspect of the product?*
- *Is it ease of procurement, habit, familiarity?*
- *Is it some aspect of the service rendered?*
- *Is it a function of peer influence?*
- *Is it a mental attitude toward the product, the company, its sales force and dealers?*
- *Is it simply the fact that the customer is aware of the existence of the product, is acquainted with its advantages and is reminded to buy?*

The questions to ask and the research techniques that will provide reasonably reliable answers to these questions are well known to experienced research practitioners. Fundamental to the creative strategy for advertising agencies is the principle of determining the characteristics, buying habits, and motivations of prospects. The research report that contains answers to such questions is just the beginning of an advertising plan, not the end product.

13. What's the Message?

We now come to the heart of advertising:

> How do we best present our product in a manner which will make prospective customers more favorably disposed toward buying it? ■

Prior work on merchandise, markets and motives has been in preparation for the key objective: "What to say about the product." If that work has been done properly, the job of deciding key advertising messages will become greatly simplified. To illustrate:

Example 3: Gasoline

The products are gasoline, motor oil, and accessories (tires, batteries, etc.). The broad marketing objective: to increase the number of regular and occasional patrons of the company's service stations and thereby increase the sales of gasoline, motor oil, accessories and, ultimately, profits. For this example, other retail outlets, such as auto supply stores and supermarkets with automotive sections, are excluded.

Research under "motives" shows that the number-one factor in regular patronage is "convenience," "friendly and efficient service," "checking under the hood," "checking tire pressure," and "clean rest rooms." Product attributes such as octane rating, quick starting, and price are found to be low on consumers' lists because they regard the several leading brands pretty much on a par.

Now, before jumping to the conclusion to select "friendly, efficient service" as a basic advertising message, it would be wise to check the reality of that assertion. If an impartial survey shows that the company's service station attendants are untidy, unfriendly and inefficient, it does not indicate a job for advertising, but rather, one for personnel selection and training. If the rest rooms and the general appearance of the stations are unclean and uninviting, it would certainly be a great mistake to claim otherwise and call this defect to the attention of the consumer. Advertising "friendly and efficient service," given such circumstances, would be counterproductive.

Let's assume that the company, in light of this information, has gone on a "spruce up" and continuing maintenance campaign and now has a real and worthwhile message to convey to the motoring public throughout its areas of distribution. Let's further assume that research has uncovered three important non-overlapping market targets. While the advertising messages overlap, the focus may differ for each:

Market Target	Message(s)
A. 40,000,000 men motorists	Friendly, fast, efficient service
B. 30,000,000 women motorists	Clean, inviting stations
C. 5,500,000 men motorists who own late model cars of makes requiring high octane gas	Quick acceleration and non-polluting anti-knock features

Media

Now we have the kind of target information that experienced media people, in conjunction with creative directors, can go to work on. They might recommend spot TV, women's magazines and spot radio as the most effective and economical way to get messages across to target markets A and B. Or, they might propose a schedule of special-interest magazines, radio and selected newspapers or direct mail for market C. Then again, they might recommend a single medium such as network TV or radio, with messages devoted to each of these copy themes.

In recent years technological advances in both print and electronic media have given advertisers more flexibility in their uses. With print media, advertisers may use different copy in reaching people in small segments of the market defined on a geographic basis through the use of concurrent Zip code editions.

Depending upon the theme of a telecast—such as "rock and roll," popular music, classical music, news and commentary, and sports—different commercials can be interspersed, not only on a geographic basis but also on a time basis, such as daytime, early evening, prime time, or late evening. The point is that media recommendations and copy treatment, tailored to a defined market and stating a relevant message for that market, can be far more meaningful and efficient.

It is not enough to say, "I recommend that we spend X% in magazines, Y% in newspapers, and Z% in network TV." We must ask these questions: "Why this particular allocation of expenditures? Are there any facts and logic to back it up?" We know that media recommendations *can* be founded on fact and logic. There is perhaps no other area of advertising with such a large body of reliable statistical information. That is why it is so important that media professionals be given defined advertising goals. Then they can produce, in return, alternate courses of action and evaluate the economic efficiency of each alternative. On-target media selection, like on-target messages, can effect large economies in the marketing budget.

14. Buying Attitude Benchmark

> If we could first know where we are and whither we are tending, we could better judge what to do and how to do it. ■

This quotation from Abraham Lincoln can be applied to advertising. Out of our research (into markets, motives, and messages) we can now establish what we shall call the "buying attitude benchmark." It tells us where we stand today in the minds of the particular audience we want to reach with respect to the particular message we want to register, and to measure its progress over time.

Example 4: Compact Car

Our hypothetical product is a make of compact car. We have thoroughly studied the market and buying motives. We feel we know the reasons that influence people to buy our make as well as competitive makes: economy, styling, riding qualities, safety, etc. We have learned that we have one decided advantage over competing makes—roominess. Our car has 3 inches more legroom, 1½ inches more headroom, and 2 inches greater seat width. Research shows that roominess is extremely important to the purchaser, especially to families with children. Now the key question is:

> How many prospective purchasers currently associate our make with roominess? ■

Let's assume a survey showed the following results in answer to the question, "Which one of these makes of cars do you most associate with roominess?"

Make A	30%
Make B	15
Make C	5
Make D	40
Don't know	10
	100%

Make A (that's us) shows up better than the others because people have discovered this feature for themselves, or because dealers have stressed it or proud owners have bragged about it. In our past advertising, this advantage has been a minor point in the copy.

A decision is made that this advantage will be the main theme of our advertising. We will direct our communicative skills and resources toward one major objective: increasing the number of people who have received the message, "Make A is the roomiest compact of them all."

How much can the 30% be increased? Over what period of time? What weight of effort will be required? These are matters of experimentation, experience and judgment. With a given expenditure, we might expect a 10 percentage point increase in a year in the number of people who get the message. A more ambitious goal, calling for larger expenditure, might be to go from 30% to 50% in one year. Pre-testing, advertising weight tests, and test market research can aid in setting realistic goals. The key principles are:

1. That a benchmark be established against which progress in communicating a defined message to a defined audience can be measured.

2. That a prediction be made of anticipated progress with a given amount and type of advertising and media plan.

Advertising people say, "For a million dollars, we expect to get this message through to an additional one million logical prospects, at a cost of $1 each." They take a calculated risk, even after the test-market research. Feedback from their national ongoing research program tells them more accurately just how "risky" their initial "calculated risk" was. It thus provides a basis for business judgment.

This prediction is similar to a "predicted log" in which a sailor says: "Considering wind and wave and current and speed of hull, I expect to arrive at a certain place at a certain time."

Part Three

The Meaning of Measured Advertising Results

Not size of audience exposed to ads...

Not noting, reading, listening, and viewing...

Not what people say they like or dislike about specific advertising...

But the changes that occur in attitude and behavior as a result of advertising. This is the meaning of measured advertising results.

15. The Meaning of Measured Advertising Results

"Measured advertising results," as used here, refers to the *systematic evaluation of the degree to which the advertising succeeded in accomplishing predetermined advertising goals.* The broad field of advertising research has many facets. Some of the principal categories are:

- *Audience Research:* in which those exposed to an ad are enumerated. This category includes surveys of the number of people who saw and read ads in print media and the number of viewers or listeners to television programs, radio programs, or commercials.

- *Media Research:* in which the size and characteristics of the audience reached by a particular medium are analyzed.

- *Copy Research:* in which advertisements are exposed to a representative target audience (readers, viewers, listeners), generally in advance of a full-scale advertising effort, and in which the reactions of that audience are evaluated.

These are valuable tools for advertising practitioners. They enable them to design and select advertising messages and media with greater attention, interest, impact, and retention value. But—essential as they are—such measurement tools are not the focus of this book. Here we are concerned with the end *results* of advertising—the extent to which the advertising succeeds in accomplishing what is set out to do.

The purpose of an advertisement is not just to get itself seen, nor to get itself heard or read. The purpose of an advertisement is to convey information and attitudes about a product (service, company, cause) in such a way that the consumer or targeted recipient will be more favorably disposed toward it. In general, the purpose of an advertisement is to bring about changes in a person's knowledge, attitude, and *behavior* with respect to the purchase of a product.

Clearly, an ad must be seen before it can be read. A viewer must physically be present to receive a television commercial. While *traffic counts* of the number of people who are exposed to ads are necessary and helpful, they do not go far enough. In addition, we need to know:

- How many *more* people are *more acutely aware* of our brand or company name after being exposed to our advertising?

- How many *more* people comprehend the features, advantages, and benefits of the product or service because of the advertising?

- How many *more* people are favorably disposed (objectively and subjectively) toward the purchase of the product or service?

- How many *more* people have gone the whole route— by visiting a showroom, or asking for, or reaching for the product?

The purpose of commercial advertising, *ultimately*, is to generate action—buy action. However, we cannot measure the pulling power of advertising solely in terms of buying action taken. Nor do we learn as much as we could about how advertising works.

A *measurement gap* exists, showing schematically in Exhibit C:

Exhibit C Measurement Gap

Exposure	*The Measurement Gap*	*Action*
Advertising audience measurement	Increased awareness Increased comprehension (of benefits) Increased conviction	Purchase of product (or other desired action)

With defined and agreed-upon goals, we can come closer to determining the extent to which people are *influenced* by advertising instead of being content with measurements that do little more than tell us how many people *are exposed*— and how often—to a particular advertisement.

Lest the purpose of this last statement be misconstrued, it should be emphatically stated that exploration into these "gap" areas does not imply lessened effort in the more established areas of advertising audience measurement. We will continue to need analyses of the number of people who are exposed to advertisements. Audience research should continue to grow in use and importance, especially as it moves beyond traditional measured media to advertising associated with special events, like the Olympics, concerts, or various sporting events.

[The word *advertising* is unfortunately limiting. It generally refers to sponsored media communications—radio, television, print, billboards and the like. There should be a broader reference. It would be better called *communications*. Sponsored advertising can be powerful, as we all know. Concurrently, we also know that endorsement by an independent (or seemingly independent) third party, such as Wimbledon, United Airlines, Disney, the Smithsonian, the Houston Astrodome, is inherently more credible, though it may literally "say" less in its message: it only exhibits the product or the brand name in the context of the institution or event. Actually, saying nothing, just being seen at Wimbledon or Disneyland speaks loudly in favor of the brand as well as the institution. (Levitt, 1990)]

If we look back at advertising in the 1920s, we find a period when advertisers had virtually no way to tell what they received for what they spent in advertising. The founding of the Audit Bureau of Circulations in 1914 was a great step forward; for the first time, advertisers had reliably audited counts of how many advertising impressions were printed and distributed.

By the 1940s, new and more advanced services were developed to meet advertisers' growing demands. Radio and TV rating services and audience measurement devices became available to tell advertisers how many people viewed, read or listened to their advertising. The circulation audit did not decline when these new advances took place.

Nor does measuring people's *exposure* to advertising completely fulfill today's increased demands as to "how" and "why" advertising works. Rather than be replaced, it will be supplemented by future additional research into what happens when people read, view, or listen to advertising messages. How do these cumulate, how are they blended with other stimuli and ultimately translated into buying action?

16. Four Stages of Commercial Communication

All advertisers who use commercial communications that aim at the ultimate objective of a sale of their products or services recognize that the consumer is confronted with many brands of the same or similar products. The communications' task is basically to carry the prospect through these four phases:

- Awareness: *Prospects must first be* aware *of the existence of a brand or company.*

- Comprehension: *They must have a* comprehension *of what the product is and what it will do for them.*

- Conviction: *They must arrive at a mental disposition or* conviction *to buy the product.*

- Action: *Finally, they must stir themselves to* action.

This succession, perhaps in different words, is as old as advertising, selling and other forms of persuasive communication.

Each level or stage has associated with it a probability of purchase of the advertised brand. Thus, even though the final "action" stage carries with it the highest probability of purchase, a prospect does not necessarily have to go through all four stages in order to consummate a purchase.

Many products and brands purchased by consumers attain only the first or second levels. This often occurs when the brand selection is not completely discretionary. For example, in a restaurant the brand of wine one drinks may be a function of availability and not necessarily of choice. To the motorist whose gas tank is approaching "E" any brand of gasoline available may suffice.

As previously discussed, to measure the accomplishment of our communication efforts, we must have a *benchmark* against which to measure that accomplishment. Prior to an advertising campaign, we should establish the following (through consumer research data):

1. How many (of the target audience) have heard about or are aware of the existence of our product or service, company, or the particular idea(s) we wish to advance in our advertising?

2. How many comprehend the particular points we wish to convey?

3. How many are favorably disposed toward its purchase?

4. How many have taken the desired action (made a purchase, visited a dealer, asked for a demonstration, requested literature, or asked a representative to call)?

The job of the advertising-marketing planner is determine *what* is to be measured, leaving methodology to the professional researcher. Some simplified examples will serve to illustrate this "before" and "after" measurement process.

Toothpaste

	Before Advertising Campaign	After Advertising Campaign
Aware of brand name:		
Unaided recall	20%	30%
Aided recall	40%	65%
Comprehend messages:		
Message A	6%	7%
Message B	10%	20%
Message C	8%	12%
Favorably disposed to buy	4%	7%
Demonstrated action	2%	4%

Industrial Chemical Division

	Before Advertising Campaign	After Advertising Campaign
Aware of corporate name	85%	88%
Aware of fact that corporation is a leading supplier of industrial chemicals	15%	25%
Comprehend messages:		
Message A	11%	12%
Message B	4%	6%
Message C	5%	12%
Favorably disposed to buy or inquire about	5%	9%
Have taken some action leading to inquiry or purchase	3%	5%

The purpose of advertising is to bring about a change in a state of mind toward the purchase of a product. Rarely is a single advertisement powerful enough to move a prospect from a complete state of unawareness to a condition of action. Rarely can a salesperson take an unknown product into a new territory and come back the first day with a book full of orders. A measure of advertising accomplishment could be measured in terms of the extent to which it moves people from one stage to another stage resulting in an increasing probability of purchase.

In the first example, the product is a toothpaste which is relatively new to the market, made from "all natural ingredients." In the second example, the industrial chemical division of a corporation more widely known for the manufacture of a line of steel-related products was seeking to increase the awareness and knowledge of the industrial chemical division and its products.

The next ad, the next sales call, the next point-of-purchase exposure or the next time the need arises may be the incremental force that moves the prospect to action.

We should not expect product advertising to do more than it is uniquely qualified to do—to convey information or create a frame of mind about a product and to stimulate action that may lead to a sale.

17. Measuring Penetration of the Key Advertising Message(s)

If we want to measure the results of advertising, the key message(s) must be designed in measurable terms. Let's consider the process in terms of an example.

Example 5: Cooking Oil

Research (under MARKETS on page 27) shows that the total (household) market is actually composed of several markets:

1. Households which use cooking oil for salads.
2. Households which use cooking oil for baking.
3. Households which use cooking oil for frying.

Research into markets has further shown that the company's product, Brand *A*, is doing very nicely in share of market for uses 1 and 2. Growth opportunities are forecast as "moderate." Market 3—use of cooking oil for frying—shows significant growth potential for the company because of a unique product claim. Furthermore, competition for this potential market is not from competitive cooking oil brands, as might be supposed, but from other products used for frying such as emulsified vegetable oil, shortening, lard, butter, and margarine, as shown by the following fictitious example:

Use of Oils and Fats in Households

| | End Use by Consumer | | |
	Salads	Baking	Frying
Total industry (gallons)	40,000,000	25,000,000	20,000,000
Share of total industry			
Brand *A*	50%	50%	10%
Competing oils	30%	30%	10%
Balance of industry (shortening, margarine, etc.)	20%	20%	80%

The fact-gathering (under MERCHANDISE on page 27) has brought out another point of potential importance. Laboratory analysis has indicated that the product contains no cholesterol while most competing products used for frying, such as shortening, lard and butter, contain significant amounts. Research into the habits, attitudes and motives of consumers indicates a concern about the cholesterol content in foods.

The Message

The central advertising message now comes through clearly— a cooking oil product with an established brand equity that does not contain cholesterol. Further research on shopping habits has indicated that homemakers tend to buy cholesterol-free brands in other product categories. The creative advertising specialists—copywriters, art directors, and TV specialists—now have sharply targeted goals to shoot at.

Media

Similarly, when we go to another group of specialists in advertising and say, "This is the specific audience I want to reach with this message," they can select media skillfully and effectively. They can figure the alternate costs of magazines, newspapers, and television. They can estimate relative effectiveness and cost per delivered message and recommend the type and timing of media with greater confidence and authority.

With these market facts and strategy, it now becomes possible to set measurable advertising goals. Let's assume the following is agreed upon on the basis of past experience, research, and judgment as a reasonable expectancy:

To communicate the "no cholesterol" feature of Brand *A* to 50% of the homemakers who use some kind of product for frying, within two years.

If this message is communicated effectively, we should also expect to see an increase in the number of people who *try* Brand *A* for this reason.

The Benchmark

Prior to the initiation of the advertising campaign, which will feature this unique selling proposition (USP) for Brand *A*, a benchmark study is undertaken to determine the uses of oils and fats in households.

Use of Oils and Fats in Households

	Benchmark Survey	Post-Advertising Survey
Number who use shortening, margarine, cooking oil, etc. for frying	20,000,000	26,000,000
Number who associate Brand *A* with "no cholesterol" feature	500,000*	15,000,000
Number who have *used* Brand *A* at some time for frying	5,000,000	10,000,000
Number who *regularly* use Brand *A* for frying	2,500,000	5,000,000

*Some consumers will mistakenly make that association even prior to any advertising. This is known as "noise," which is present in any communication system.

Post-Advertising Survey

We will assume that a year's advertising campaign focusing on this theme has run at a cost of $10,000,000. A survey is then conducted to measure results. The results are shown above, in the column headed "Post-Advertising Survey." Net increases are as follows:

• Increase in number of people who use shortening, margarine, cooking oil, etc.	6,000,000
• Increase in number who "got the message"	14,500,000
• Increase in number who tried Brand *A*	5,000,000
• Increase in regular users of Brand *A* for frying	2,500,000

Economic Evaluation

- *Did this advertising campaign pay out?*
- *Should we increase our expenditure?*
- *Should we continue with present theme and media?*

We can now make calculated business judgments on these key management decisions. Let's say that the average regular user consumes $20 worth of the product annually, on which the manufacturer makes a gross profit of $4. Actual additional tonnage moved during the calendar year brought an additional profit of $10 million against an advertising cost of $10 million. These figures might lead some to conclude that a break-even situation was hardly worth the effort, until we consider other factors:

- The data indicated that Brand *A* doubled the number of its regular users in the "cooking oils used in frying" segment of the market. Suppose the average life of a converted user proves to be five years. On this basis, the advertising will eventually pay out 4 to 1 after breaking even for the first year.
- Millions of people who were unaware of the brand— or only casually aware of it—now have a mental

image of its benefits. With further stimulation, some can be moved into the "frying" category. During the first year's campaign, we already note an increase of 6,000,000 homemakers who use shortening, margarine, cooking oil, etc. for frying.

- The company, through this campaign, was able to expand its distribution (by 30,000 retail outlets) and improve its point-of-purchase display.

- Past experience indicates that without this "expanded" advertising campaign, the company would normally expect to spend at least half this volume of advertising just to keep pace with competition and maintain its established share of industry. Hence, only half the advertising costs should be weighed against *increased* sales.

With these facts in hand, along with the addition of competitive marketing intelligence, we can conduct our economic evaluation more effectively and modify our future marketing plans, including advertising expenditure, advertising theme, media mix, and line extensions.

18. Can It Be Measured?

A good question to ask about every proposed ad or campaign is: *"Can its impact be measured?"* If the answer is "no," chances are the communication objective has not been clarified.

Chances are also that advertisers, no matter how devoted they may be to the philosophy of measured results, will not, in actual practice, measure every ad or even every campaign. Time, manpower, and cost must be considered. We don't measure *everything* that is done in personal selling, or product development, or pricing. Objective judgment should be applied to the cost/benefit relationship of such measurement.

However, regardless of whether an advertisement or campaign is slated for measurement, it is good practice to specify *how* it can be measured. Inability to answer the question, "How can it be measured?" is a strong signal that the purpose of the ad is not clearly defined.

19. Tracking Advertising Performance

In the interests of simplicity, most of the examples in this book illustrate a "before and after" situation.

For example:

	Before Advertising Campaign	After Advertising Campaign
Aware of fact that steel corporation X is also a leading supplier of industrial chemicals	15%	30%
Associate Brand *A* of cooking oil with "no cholesterol"	500,000	15,000,000

In actual practice, though, companies with well-organized, long-range advertising research operations continually conduct studies of share in mind, message penetration and product usage. Using independent consumer cross sections and other research techniques, "trend lines" can be established that show changes in consumer knowledge and attitude on an annual, quarterly or even monthly basis. A number of leading advertisers use continuing research for "tracking advertising performance" much as a meteorologist uses a barometer and other devices for tracking high- and low-pressure areas and making weather predictions. Many advertisers will continue to take measurements well beyond the "after" period in order to evaluate the carryover advertising effects of a campaign once it has ceased.

You should note that most of the examples given throughout the book illustrate *increases* in the level of "awareness," "comprehension," "conviction" or "action." Actually, a company doing a truly outstanding advertising job may be doing well to *maintain* its already high level. For example, one industrial advertiser, through years of effective advertising efforts, has achieved a corporate identity of 95%. A consumer goods advertiser, after many years of persistent advertising, has achieved an 80% association between their brand name and the number-one product benefit claim.

Considering the forces at work that "erode" identity and preference (about three million new consumers currently entering the market yearly; the countervailing forces of both "memory lapse" and competition), advertisers may find it necessary to increase their expenditures each year simply to maintain their present share of the consumer's attention. (See Section 24 for more details.)

Continuing trend information in the area of communication effectiveness enables advertisers to make more intelligent decisions regarding long-held enigmas of advertising:

- How much to spend?
- How long before the advertising goals are met?
- Whether to "maintain" or "switch" themes?
- What is the relative media effectiveness?

The following chart demonstrates how a marketer of a leading brand of coffee with a unique roasting process tracked the progress of an intensive campaign to enhance the reputation of this blend of premium coffee. While coffees in general are blended from different types of coffee beans and then roasted, this product's manufacturing process roasted the different types of coffee beans to their optimum temperature and then blended them. Though this brand held a good position in the market, the advertising goal was to market it as the outstanding blend on account of this feature. The campaign—which started with intensive advertising of this feature in both print and television—leveled off during the fall months and was terminated after Thanksgiving Day. Marketing measurements were initiated at the start of the campaign and carried over after advertising ceased. The plotted line shows the progress in the association of the brand with the unique pre-blend roasting procedure. The advertising goal statement (Exhibit D) is indicated below. The media schedule and the budgeted advertising dollars that accompany advertising goal statements have not been included:

Exhibit D   Statement of Goal—Brand *A* Coffee

Target Market:	Primary Shoppers 30–55; Household Income $35,000
Size of Target:	27,000,000 Primary Shoppers
Objective:	To Increase Awareness that Brand *A* Uses the "Roast and Blend" Process in Manufacturing Its Coffee
Measuring Instrument:	"Which One of the Following Brands Do You Associate with the Roast and Blend Process?"

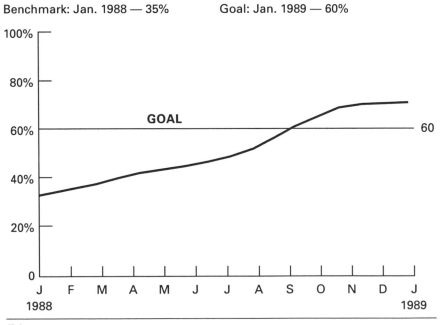

Benchmark: Jan. 1988 — 35%   Goal: Jan. 1989 — 60%

Part Four

Advertising's Purpose in Your Business

Here we enquire: *Is there a basic philosophy regarding the purpose of advertising in your company? Is this philosophy understood and accepted by all those who influence and approve key advertising decisions?*

20. Understanding Advertising's Purpose

An example of the many different people involved in the creation and approval of advertising is shown in the organization chart on the preceding page (Exhibit E). The boxes show only the managers of the various departments in the agency and advertiser organization. Actually, several people in each department may be concerned with the advertising for a particular product. Small advertisers may have a handful of different people concerned, while larger advertisers may have dozens involved in advertising a single product, or hundreds concerned with an entire product line. Do all of these people hold a common understanding of advertising's purpose?

We have already indicated what the result would be if one were to conduct a survey among these individuals asking: "What are we trying to accomplish with this campaign or ad for this product at this time?" Similar diversity of opinion would undoubtedly result if the survey asked the more general question: "What is advertising's purpose in our company?"

The President may lean strongly toward building a "corporate image." The Sales Manager may regard advertising as a means of getting larger orders from retailers. Financial people may regard advertising as an expense, chargeable to a given fiscal period. The Advertising Manager or the agency account executive may regard advertising as an investment, directed toward building the brand's equity and increasing share of market.

Gaining a *common* understanding of advertising's contribution is critical to advertiser and agency. Too often, those who influence and approve key advertising decisions have had little direct advertising experience. However, it is reassuring to note that the final decision-makers in U.S. industry are reaching out for a better understanding of advertising and how it can be employed most profitably in their businesses.

Exhibit E Organization Chart Showing Persons Concerned with Advertising

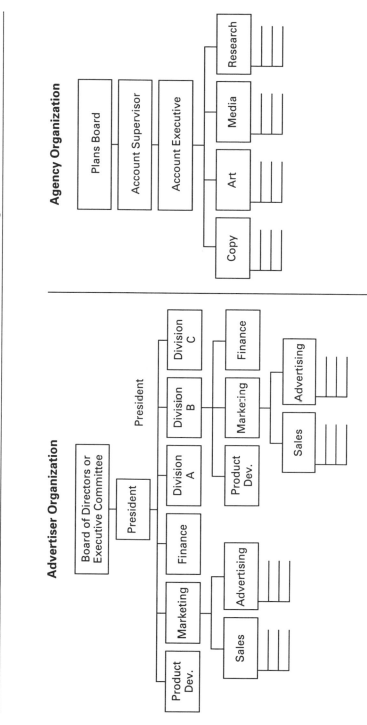

The remaining chapters in Part Four explain the advertising process—what it is and how it operates—illustrating concepts helpful in gaining a general understanding of advertising's function and contribution in various business scenarios.

21. What Is Advertising?

Advertising professionals might think it naive to ask, "What is advertising?" They may say such a question is appropriate only for students and trainees, not for experienced, sophisticated marketing and sales executives.

Yet the meaning of advertising needs to be specified, largely because different meanings frequently are attached to the terms "advertising," "sales promotion," "publicity," "selling," and "marketing." It is important that those within a given company have a common understanding of terminology. Terminology differs from industry to industry and within industries. Differences of opinion on "What is advertising?" are clearly demonstrated during budget preparation. In some companies, the advertising budget includes only paid space and TV or radio time. In others, it includes sales literature, promotional and point-of-sale materials, price sheets, publicity releases, house organs, trade releases, trade shows, employee communications, etc. (A possibly apocryphal story in the industry deals with an advertising manager who thought it was going a little too far for corporate to charge his budget for repair and maintenance of the clock on the branch office building that carried the company's logo.)

In some companies, advertising includes all forms of mass paid communication directed toward influencing the *end consumer*, whereas sales promotion includes those forms of mass communication directed toward informing and influencing the *channels of distribution:* salespeople, distributors, and dealers. In other companies, sales promotion includes mass communication materials (literature, catalogs, displays, and films) used *by* the channels of distribution (salespeople, retailers) as selling aids. Hence, a piece of product literature mailed directly to a customer is advertising while literature distributed by the sales force or dealer is sales promotion. Still another (and perhaps the most traditional) distinction between advertising and sales promotion is that advertising consists of time, space and preparatory costs in *commissionable media.* All other mass commercial communications are regarded as sales promotion. Some industries and channels of distribution use the term "sales promotion" to refer to any and all activities promoting sales including: premium offers and other special inducements to consumers, special price offers, sales drives, and contests, all in addition to advertising. Under such usage, the term "sales promotion" becomes synonymous with "merchandising" and even "marketing." In the early 1960s, mass communication budgets were dominated by commissionable advertising. Today the situation has changed. In 1991, for example, the packaged goods industry spent over $70 billion on advertising and promotion. Of that, over 40 percent was in trade promotion at the retail level, almost 30 percent was spent on consumer promotion, and just over 30 percent was devoted to measured media advertising.

Larry Light, Chairman of the Coalition for Brand Equity, points out that advertising and promotion working together tend to produce enduring, profitable brand growth.

> Advertising helps to build and reinforce a quality, differentiated brand reputation and as relative advertising weight goes up, so does market rank.
>
> Advertising helps get a brand into the consideration set. But here is where promotion plays its most significant role: You need both advertising

and promotion to achieve and maintain a profitable, market leader position.

How do advertising and promotion help to build premium quality, differentiated, market dominant, enduring, profitable brands? The answer is clear: Advertising helps to build rank of mind. Promotion helps to turn rank of mind into rank of market. Advertising is important. So is promotion. To become a market leader, promotion is also necessary. ∎

The reasons for the use of promotions are as varied as the promotions themselves. Money for trade promotion is used to open channels of distribution, to obtain retailer cooperation, for increased shelf facings, for dealer contents and advertising allowances, etc. In recent years, manufacturers have emphasized consumer-oriented promotions in the form of price reductions, the use of coupons, and consumer contests.

Promotions can achieve fast response by inducing action, resulting in an anticipated increase in sales. Consumer-oriented promotions seldom aim at product or brand characteristics, but are mainly concerned with price benefits. It is generally agreed, however, that a manufacturer will not use consumer-oriented promotions unless a sold advertising base has been established. While brand equity is an important asset for price promotions, some marketers feel that the promotions themselves may erode brand equity and have a tendency to denigrate brands in a product category to commodity status competing only on the basis of price. This poses an interesting paradox since the fundamental purpose of brand advertising is to reduce price sensitivity.

Currently, interest on consumer promotions has been aided by two interrelated factors—the speed of consumers' reaction and by the speed of measurement at retail. With the general use of scanner-based data bases in food and drug stores, the short-term measures of market actions can be assessed. Often they do show that price promotions have an immediate effect on sales. However, the long-term effects and true profitability measures are more difficult to assess.

Returning to our question, "What is advertising?" we start with the obvious fact that advertising is a form of communication. Communication has been defined as, "all means by which one mind affects another." Letters or personal calls by salespeople to customers are communicators. The difference is that advertising is *mass* communication. So is a story in a newspaper or magazine, or a play on television. So is a sermon or a political speech. As a matter of fact, all of the fine arts—music, poetry, painting, drama—are forms of communication. They convey a frame of mind. By whatever means, these art forms make contact and thereby transmit a mood or "message" from one human mind to another.

We begin to separate advertising from the many other forms of communication when we add the term "commercial" or "paid." Advertising is paid for by a sponsor who expects to induce some kind of action on the part of the reader, listener or viewer that will be beneficial to the advertiser. To sum up in a definition:

> Advertising is mass, paid communication, the ultimate purpose of which is to impart information, develop attitude, and *induce* action beneficial to the advertiser (generally the sale of a product or service). ∎

Paid political announcements, recruitment ads, even a "lost dog" ad in the newspapers' classified columns are all advertising. They are mass communications, paid for by a sponsor who wishes to achieve some end: the election of a candidate, the hiring of personnel, or the recovery of the family pet. The bulk of all advertising *aims* toward the ultimate sale of a product or service—the area of advertising as a marketing force with which we are primarily concerned.

22. How the Advertising Process Works

The ultimate purpose of most advertising is to help bring about the sale of a product or service. To add to our further understanding of this, one can ask two very simple and obvious questions:

1. *When? (Speed of reaction to the advertising)*
2. *How much of the sales-making load is to be carried by advertising?*

Look at the first question. The speed of reaction to the advertising, as well as the nature of the reaction, varies according to other factors.

A department store runs an ad in the evening paper announcing a sensational sale of an item. Next morning, people are lined up waiting for the doors to open. Hours later, the clerks may be saying, "Sorry, we're sold out." These same clerks may sometimes "turn off" customers responding to the advertised sale by this store. Advertising may have been too successful.

A corporation runs a "corporate image" ad aimed at prospective employees at the student level. Ten years later, the same students who read the ad may apply for jobs, or they may specify the company's products on a purchase order, or they may buy some of the company's stock for their families.

The time objective of most advertising falls somewhere between these two extremes. Advertisers of automobiles, insurance, farm equipment, or machine tools do not expect people to rush out and buy their products. But they do expect to move prospects somewhat closer to purchasing the product. In short, advertising's job is to increase *propensity* to buy—to move prospects closer to a purchase. If one out of ten or even one out of a hundred of the people who are exposed to the ads take *near-term buying action*, the ad campaign may be considered a huge success.

Now examine the second question: *"How much of the sales-making load is to be carried by advertising?"*

At one extreme, we have mail-order advertisers who would answer, "100%," because advertising is their only commercial communication force. At the other extreme is the industrial company in which personal selling is the key sales-making force. Advertising for this company assists by carrying part of the communications workload. One corporation, manufacturing a line of both consumer and industrial products, figured the advertising-to-sales ratio for its products varied from a high of 18% to a low of under 1%.

Between such extremes, there is a wide range of products where advertising is blended with packaging, promotion, price and personal selling, with all of these forces contributing to the consummation of a sale.

To repeat, two variables are at work:

1. The speed of reaction to the advertising.
2. The share of the sales-making load to be carried by advertising.

The Communications Spectrum

The concept of the "Marketing Communications Spectrum" (briefly referred to in Chapter 16) offers a starting approach to solving the problem. This is a concept of applied common sense. It breaks the process into logical and comprehensible steps. It begins with the obvious assumption that advertising is a communication force. It does not physically impel the consumer toward the purchase of goods; rather, its purpose is to create a state of mind conducive toward such behavior. Simply, advertising is one of several communication forces which (acting singly or in combination) move the consumer through successive levels or steps of the communications spectrum. These levels (shown in Exhibit F) are UNAWARENESS, AWARENESS, COMPREHENSION, CONVICTION, and ACTION. Let's discuss the levels.

Exhibit F   Marketing Communications Spectrum

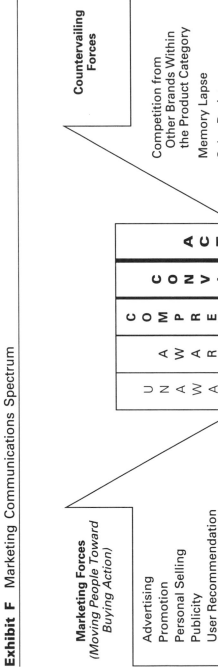

Marketing Forces
(Moving People Toward Buying Action)

Advertising
Promotion
Personal Selling
Publicity
User Recommendation
Product Design
Availability
Display
Price
Packaging
Exhibits

Countervailing Forces

Competition from
Other Brands Within
the Product Category
Memory Lapse
Sales Resistance
Market Attrition
Competition from Other
Product Categories
Other Environmental Factors

ACTION

CONVICTION

COMPREHENSION

AWARENESS

UNAWARENESS

The starting level of this communications spectrum is UNAWARENESS. Here are the people who have never heard of our product or company. Any messages about the product have not penetrated to the point where the consumer recognizes or recalls the brand or company name. Of course, it is conceivable that people will buy products or vote for candidates whose names are unknown to them, but chances are that such a product would actually make a few sales and such a candidate would get few votes. As a bare minimum then, we strive to bring the consumer to the next level, AWARENESS.

Beyond AWARENESS is COMPREHENSION. In this state, consumers not only are aware of the product or service, but know the brand name, recognize the package or trademark, and, in addition, possess some degree of comprehension of what the product is and does. They may say, "Brand *A* is a headache remedy that the maker claims will give fast relief and will not upset the stomach," or "The *B* company is a manufacturer of earthmoving equipment that will scoop up 20 tons in one bite."

CONVICTION, the next level of the spectrum, can be illustrated by a consumer who says, "Brand *B* is the name of a new synthetic fiber made by the "X" Company. Garments made of this fiber are wrinkle resistant, wear longer and hold their shape better. I buy clothing made from this fiber whenever I can." Advertisers characterize these as the intrinsic properties of their products. Conviction may also be illustrated by a consumer who prefers a particular brand of deodorant on a more subjective basis or one who prefers a particular brand of mouthwash on more of a psychological basis than a product-specific one. Advertisers characterize these as the extrinsic properties of their products.

Finally, if the marketing forces come to bear fruit, there is ACTION. Here, consumers have made overt moves toward the purchase of the product. They may have visited a dealer's showroom and asked for a demonstration. Or they may have asked for literature or for a salesperson to call. Or they may have asked for or reached for the brand at the retail store.

Ultimate consummation of the sale may go beyond the power of advertising. For instance, the dealer did not have the model in stock, a trade-in allowance may have been too low, a salesperson may have failed to follow up the lead, a price might be considered too high, or a product may lack appeal when physically examined. Nonetheless, advertising induced action.

Advertising performs its role when it contributes to moving the consumer through one or more levels of the spectrum: awareness of the existence of the product, comprehension of its features and advantages, rational or emotional conviction of its benefits and, finally, action that leads to a sale. This cannot be used as a measure of the effect of the advertising. Later, we will discuss how the effect can be determined.

Consumer studies indicate that at each level or step there is some probability of a purchase and, as the consumer progresses from "unawareness" to "action," that probability increases. For some products, the total amount of purchasing at a given stage (which equals the number of consumers at the stage multiplied by the probability of purchasing at that stage) may be equal to or larger than gross purchases at some of the more advanced stages. This may occur because the number of consumers at the less advanced stage may be considerably larger than the number of consumers at the more advanced stage. Generally, as the stages progress, there is an inverse relationship between purchase probability and the size of these potential consumer groups. Purchase probabilities tend to increase, while the number of potential consumers at each stage tends to decrease.

Considering these two tendencies simultaneously, many marketers and advertisers visualize the spectrum as a funnel instead of a ladder. The wide mouth of the funnel designates unawareness and the corresponding large number of consumers at this stage, while the narrow end designates action. The aim of advertising is to expedite the flow of consumers through the funnel. A funnel flow for a typical product is shown in Exhibit G.

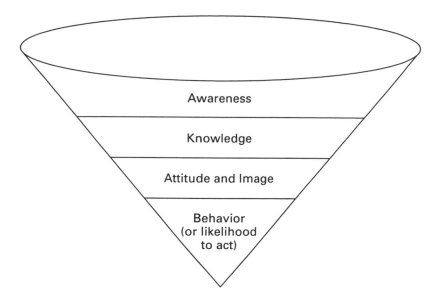

Awareness

Knowledge

Attitude and Image

Behavior
(or likelihood
to act)

The sizes of the sections of the funnel and their respective purchase probabilities will vary for different products and services and at different times. All are amenable to change depending upon the product itself, as well as on the advertising focus.

The Marketing Communications Mix

Advertising is but one of several forces contributing to awareness, comprehension, conviction, and action. Those other forces vary, depending upon whether a "consumer" or "industrial" product or service is being advertised. Forces may include: person-to-person selling, the recommendation of another user or a retailer, or publicity and various other forms of mass communication such as displays, exhibits, films, or literature.

Rarely does a single communication force move a prospect through the entire communications cycle. Exceptions do exist though. Mail-order advertising can and does move a reader through the entire spectrum from unawareness to a cash-in-advance sale—action—in a few hundred words. Door-to-door salespeople and street-corner demonstrators often sell such items as kitchen utensils, cosmetics, or brushes to consumers in a few minutes of persuasive selling.

But the use of advertising or personal selling to achieve the wrapped-up, one-shot sale is but a tiny fraction of most advertising and selling efforts. More often, all forces of marketing communication work together in a "mix" or "blend" to move prospects step by step to become satisfied customers.

Thus, one purpose of advertising is to perform certain parts of the communicating job with greater economy, speed, and volume than can be accomplished through other means.

In some instances—notably consumer package goods— advertising may be called upon to carry the full marketing communications workload from awareness right through to action. Consider a product sold through self-service grocery and drug outlets. The function of today's package goods retailer is to make goods conveniently available and to provide facilities for the physical exchange of goods and money. In this situation, advertising is the major communicative force between manufacturer and consumer.

In other product lines, notably industrial goods, advertising is generally a complementary communicative force. The typical company salesperson calling on industrial accounts may make only three or four calls a day. If we subtract the time spent in filling out sales forms and expense accounts, behind a steering wheel, in reception rooms, in handling various service duties and in building friendly relations, the actual face-to-face time spent in *presenting the merits of the product* to the customer is small. The cost per sales call and per selling minute is high; the rate of penetration of sales messages to the many thousands of buying influencers is slow. *Advertising's job is to increase the pro-ductivity of the salesperson (or sales force) by shouldering a substantial part of the communication workload.*

Falling somewhere between these two extremes just discussed are consumer durables and semidurables (autos, appliances, home furnishings, jewelry, clothing, etc.). Advertising's job? Deliver people who are informed and emotionally favorable to a brand across the retailer's threshold. One should remember that advertising informs and influences retailers as well. Of course, in any kind of product, consummation of a sale may also depend upon product appearance, price, availability in desired size, color, and other aesthetic and/or economic factors.

Advertising's job may vary with the season or the stage of a product's development. It may be to introduce a new product or display a new use for an existing one. It may be to stress specific, unique product benefits or to create a favorable emotional disposition toward a company or brand. And in some cases, advertising's primary function is simply to remind people to buy, or to stimulate impulse purchases.

> In every case, the function of advertising is to perform a commercial communication task more economically than by alternate means. ∎

Advertising Is Automated Marketing Communication

We tend to regard automation as a process applied to the factory or the office, overlooking the fact that advertising is "automated marketing communication." As such, it involves a system that consists of many components shown in the schematic diagram (Exhibit H).

All advertising executives are familiar with the components of this system. While we have concentrated on the measurement of the end product in the measurement of

Exhibit H Schematic Diagram for Advertising Communication

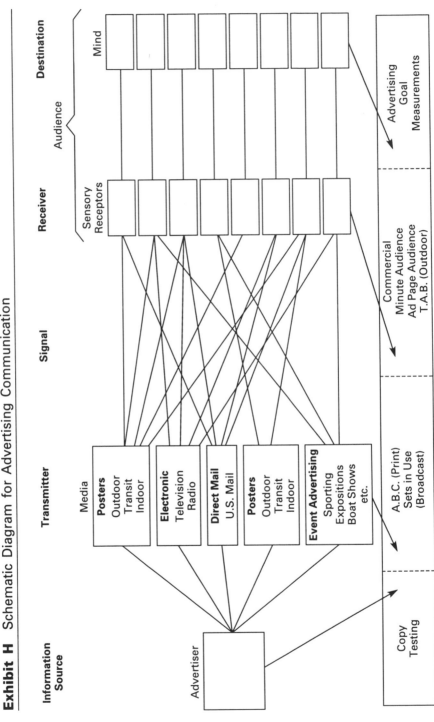

advertising goals, it should be emphasized that any unattended operating system tends to run down. At the same time, however, the system produces knowledge in the form of feedback that indicates its status and suggests ways it can be improved. Feedback checks from each of these components should be reexamined periodically.

Similarly, we approach marketing communications on a "task basis":

- What are the communicating tasks to be done?
- What parts of these tasks is advertising uniquely and economically qualified to perform?
- What is the ideal "mix" of communication forces for *each* product at each particular stage in its marketing development?

23. Marketing Mix in Action

Advertising, as one of several marketing forces, acts upon potential customers and moves them toward buying action. Seldom does a single force (such as advertising or personal selling) perform this entire task alone. And rarely is a single message powerful enough to move a prospect through the entire spectrum, from unawareness to action.

Let's look at an example of how advertising has played a part in this process. A number of years ago, an automobile manufacturer was focusing its advertising for one of its makes of cars, the NEXIS, on young male heads of household. As part of their ongoing nationwide survey, automobile attitude measurements were obtained for this group (as shown below). Six months later, in a scheduled reinterview, data on the shopping and buying behavior of this group was obtained.

Value of Preference Levels in Terms of

Probability of Purchase and Dealer Visitation

(Among young male heads of household who *purchased a new car during the past six months*)

Mutually Exclusive Response Categories	Initial Attitude Percent	Visited NEXIS Dealer	Bought NEXIS
No Mention of NEXIS	66%	1.5%	0.4%
Aware of NEXIS	14%	24.0%	5.0%
NEXIS in Buying Class, But *Not* Favorably Considered	8%	40.0%	9.0%
Favorably Considered	7%	62.0%	22.0%
NEXIS First Choice	5%	84.0%	56.0%

The results indicated that among the 5% who had six months ago considered the NEXIS as their "first choice" and bought a new car (any new car), 84% had visited a NEXIS dealer during the 6-month period while 56% actually purchased a NEXIS. Similarly, 7% of the target market initially rated the NEXIS as a "make they would favorably consider" when purchasing a new car. During the 6-month interval, some 62% of them visited a NEXIS dealer and 22% of those who rated NEXIS as a "make they would favorably consider" when purchasing a new car wound up buying a NEXIS.

The role of advertising in getting the customer to the dealer was described very clearly by Lee Iacocca during a September 1992 interview with *The Wall Street Journal:*

". . . And the best [advertising] doesn't mean you win an Emmy or something. . . . It's that the dealers immediately react and say people are talking about it and coming in. *I mean that's what advertising is supposed to do, give you a crack at some traffic . . . what the hell good is it if it doesn't help you sell cars?"* ■

Advertising Age, 9/17/92.
Interview with Lee Iacocca,
Chairman, Chrysler Corporation
(Emphasis ours).

Because a strong relationship exists between preference level and the probability of purchase, the company's marketing objective has to move prospective purchasers from the "NEXIS in Buying Class But *Not* Favorably Considered" level (where the purchase probability was .090) to the "NEXIS Favorably Considered" level (where the purchase probability was .220). An examination of how each of these two groups rated the NEXIS on over a dozen attributes is indicated by the following:

Ratings of NEXIS—By Item
(On Scale of 1–100)

Consider NEXIS to be in Their "Buying Class"		
	But Will *Not* Give It Favorable Consideration	And Will Give It Favorable Consideration	Difference
Smooth Riding	86	91	3
Styling	76	89	13
Overall Comfort	81	87	6
Handling	83	86	3
Spacious Interior	85	85	0
Luxurious Interior	79	85	6
Quality of Workmanship	80	83	3
Advanced Engineering	77	83	3
Prestige	73	82	9
Value for the Money	76	79	3
Trade-In Value	59	77	18
Cost of Upkeep and Maintenance	63	67	4
Gas Economy	58	58	0

This table shows that the principal difference between the two groups is in their image ratings of "Trade-in Value." Further study revealed that the "will not" group did not tend to associate the particular model NEXIS with the overall brand, thereby affecting its trade-in value. Thus, modifying the existing advertising campaign for NEXIS to more closely associate it with the name of its manufacturing division and its actual Blue Book Trade-in Value became the advertising objective. No attempt was made to set an advertising goal for "Styling" because it was determined that the amount of money required to improve those ratings would not be worthwhile. The same principles involved in this specific case can also be applied generally.

In some situations, advertising may be designed to work at all levels at the same time. Let's assume that the market is equally divided into the five levels shown in Exhibit I.

Let's assume that, as a result of an advertising campaign, half at each level move down one rung on the ladder. Then we would have the results shown in Exhibit J.

In this instance, advertising has worked "across the board," moving some people from unawareness to awareness, others to comprehension, conviction, and action.

Exhibit I Communications Spectrum—Equally Divided

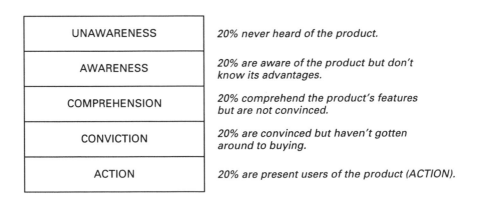

UNAWARENESS	20% never heard of the product.
AWARENESS	20% are aware of the product but don't know its advantages.
COMPREHENSION	20% comprehend the product's features but are not convinced.
CONVICTION	20% are convinced but haven't gotten around to buying.
ACTION	20% are present users of the product (ACTION).

Under certain market conditions, such as intense competition or in times of economic recession, advertising may perform a valuable economic function if it succeeds in helping a company merely *maintain its existing share of the consumer mind* or *its brand equity.*

In some entirely different situations, the force of advertising may be directed at one particular level in the spectrum, rather than "across the board." Some situations, for example, call for advertising that is entirely *action*-oriented (Exhibit K):

Exhibit J Communications Spectrum—30% Action

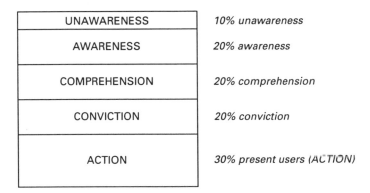

UNAWARENESS	10% unawareness
AWARENESS	20% awareness
COMPREHENSION	20% comprehension
CONVICTION	20% conviction
ACTION	30% present users (ACTION)

Exhibit K Communications Spectrum—50% Action

UNAWARENESS
AWARENESS
COMPREHENSION
CONVICTION
ACTION

For example, consider the advertising for a leading brand of razor blades. Almost everyone is acquainted with the product. And while not 100% of these people are convinced of the brand's superiority, its high market share indicates that this is not the key issue. What is advertising's job here? It may well be to *remind* people to restock their personal inventory (that is, take action). People forget to buy blades and use old blades beyond their normal product life.

See Exhibit L. A leading established brand in a highly competitive market—such as a headache remedy—might channel the bulk of its advertising efforts toward the *conviction* level of the spectrum. Advertising's job in such an example may be to demonstrate product superiority and thereby increase brand preference. Some advertisers may also utilize "comparative advertising" in this content.

Similarly, there are marketing situations, such as those for "new" new products, in which the major advertising emphasis is placed at the awareness level. After the product is introduced, the emphasis may then change from "awareness" advertising to product feature advertising.

Exhibit L Communications Spectrum—50% Conviction

24. Which of These 52 Advertising Tasks Are Important in Your Business?

Advertising may be called upon to perform a combination of different tasks that lead to the ultimate objective of a sale. The job of defining the objective is essentially deciding which of the multiplicity of communication tasks we want to accomplish through advertising.

The following checklist of 52 advertising tasks (Exhibit M) was prepared to aid those seeking a better understanding of the purpose and contribution of advertising in a business. They are not substitutes for specific measurable advertising goals. The checklist is obviously incomplete. Participants will think of additional important tasks in a particular marketing situation. But if all concerned with advertising—in the agency, advertising department, marketing department, sales, and general management—go through such a checklist and thoughtfully consider each item, the results can be positive, contributing to obtaining realistic and agreed-upon goals.

To assist in evaluating the importance of each task, a rating scale is provided in the checklist. Ratings of 0 or 1 indicate that the task is of little or no importance to the particular product line under consideration. Moderately important tasks are rated as 2 or 3. A rating of 4 or 5 indicates that the task is extremely important. A company making a diversified line of products would do well to confine the initial experiment to a single product category.

What may appear to be a mental exercise is actually a mind-opening process. Perhaps the greatest benefit to be derived from this process is the recognition that a multiplicity of communication tasks are to be performed, and that certain tasks are of paramount importance for product *A* and of lesser importance for product *B*. In short, the checklist is simply an organized way to arrive at a *priority of importance* of the various communication tasks (Exhibit M).

(This checklist is a "thought starter" in developing specific advertising objectives. It can be applied to a single ad, a campaign for each product, or it can aid in developing a company's advertising philosophy among those who create and approve advertising.)

To what extent does the advertising aim at closing an immediate sale?

	Scale of Importance					
	Not Important				Very Important	
	0	1	2	3	4	5
1. Perform the complete selling function (take the product through all the necessary steps toward a sale)?						
2. Close sales to prospects already partly sold through past advertising efforts ("Ask for the order" or "clincher" advertising)?						
3. Announce a special reason for "buying now" (price, premium, etc.)?						
4. *Remind* people to buy?						
5. Tie in with some special buying event?						
6. Stimulate impulse sales?						

OTHER TASKS:

_____

_____

Does the advertising aim at <u>near-term</u> sales by moving the prospect, step by step, closer to a sale (so that when confronted with a buying situation the customer will ask for, reach for, or accept the advertised brand)?

	Scale of Importance					
	Not Important					Very Important
	0	1	2	3	4	5

7. Create awareness of existence of product or brand?

8. Create "brand image" or favorable emotional disposition toward the brand?

9. Implant information or attitude regarding benefits and superior features of brand?

10. Combat or offset competitive claims?

11. Correct false impressions, misinformation and other obstacles to sales?

12. Build familiarity and easy recognition of package or trademark?

OTHER TASKS:

_____

_____

Does the advertising aim at building a "long-range consumer franchise?"

	Scale of Importance					
	Not Important				*Very Important*	
	0	1	2	3	4	5

13. Build confidence in company and brand which is expected to pay off in years to come?

14. Build customer demand which places company in stronger position in relation to its distribution (not at the "mercy of the marketplace")?

15. Place advertiser in position to select preferred distributors and dealers?

16. Secure universal distribution?

17. Establish a "reputation platform" for launching new brand or product lines?

18. Establish brand recognition and acceptance which will enable the company to open up new markets (geographic, price, age, sex)?

OTHER TASKS:

_____

_____

Specifically, how can advertising contribute toward increased sales?

	Scale of Importance					
	Not Important				Very Important	
	0	1	2	3	4	5

19. Hold present customers against the inroads of competition?

20. Convert competitive users to advertiser's brand?

21. Cause people to specify advertiser's brand instead of asking for product by generic name?

22. Convert nonusers of the product type to users of product and brand?

23. Make steady customers out of occasional or sporadic customers?

24. Advertise new uses of the product?

25. Persuade customers to buy larger sizes or multiple units?

26. Remind users to buy?

27. Encourage greater frequency or quantity of use?

OTHER TASKS:

_____

_____

Does the advertising aim at some specific step that leads to a sale?

Scale of Importance					
Not Important				Very Important	
0	1	2	3	4	5

28. Persuade prospect to write for descriptive literature, return a coupon, enter a contest?

29. Persuade prospect to visit a showroom, ask for a demonstration?

30. Induce prospects to sample the product (trial offer)?

OTHER TASKS:

_____

_____

How important are "supplementary benefits" of end-use advertising?

	Scale of Importance					
	Not Important				*Very Important*	
	0	1	2	3	4	5
31. Aid sales force in opening new accounts?						
32. Aid sales force in getting larger orders from wholesalers and retailers?						
33. Aid sales force in getting preferred display space?						
34. Give sales force an entrée?						
35. Build morale of company sales force?						
36. Impress the trade (causing recommendation to their customers and favorable treatment to sales force)?						
OTHER TASKS:						
_____						
_____						

Is it a task of advertising to impart information needed to consummate sales and build customer satisfaction?

	Scale of Importance					
	Not Important				Very Important	
	0	1	2	3	4	5

37. "Where to buy it" advertising?

38. "How to use it" advertising?

39. New models, features, package?

40. New prices?

41. Special terms, trade-in offers, etc.?

42. New policies (guarantees, etc.)?

OTHER TASKS:

_____

_____

To what extent does the advertising aim at building confidence and goodwill for the corporation among:

	Scale of Importance					
	Not Important				*Very Important*	
	0	1	2	3	4	5
43. Customers and potential customers?						
44. The trade (distribution, dealers, retail salespeople)?						
45. Employees and potential employees?						
46. The financial community?						
47. The public at large?						
OTHER TASKS:						

Specifically, what kind of images does the company wish to build?

	Scale of Importance					
	Not Important					Very Important
	0	1	2	3	4	5
48. Product quality, dependability?						
49. Service?						
50. Family resemblance of diversified products?						
51. Corporate citizenship?						
52. Growth, progressiveness, technical leadership?						

OTHER TASKS:

_____

_____

Part Five

Brief Examples Illustrating the Definition of Advertising Goals*

* Examples 1 through 5 are included in other parts of this book.
   Examples 6 through 19 follow.

The principles of defining advertising goals and measuring results are best understood through the review of case histories. Part Five presents brief examples of a variety of industries and marketing situations. The examples given, while drawing liberally from actual experience and practice, are "hypothetical" for several reasons. It is difficult to find enough actual examples to illustrate a wide variety of products and industries. Furthermore, companies that have put these principles into practice are, for competitive reasons, reluctant to reveal their full findings. And, finally, the authentic case history tends to become quite lengthy.

Hence, it was decided to review, in a highly condensed form, a diversity of situations using fictitious figures and product categories. In some cases, names and figures have been altered to avoid disclosure. A soup company, for example, may be changed to a soap company; machine tools may be presented as farm equipment.

Some examples are, in fact, a montage of practices drawn from several known situations. To the extent possible, these examples have been checked with representative advertisers and agencies in an effort to make them as realistic of the industry depicted as possible.

Example 6: Hosiery

Background

Market: 90 million people who customarily wear hosiery nearly every day

Marketing Goals: Establish distribution in 1200 grade A retail outlets; achieve sales volume of $15 million in three years

Advertising Goals: Introductory:

- Establish brand awareness among 60% of people in one year
- Convey message: Antifatigue benefits plus sheer beauty to 30% in one year

Once established:

- Maintain above levels of awareness and primary message registration
- Increase registration of economy message from 10% to 30%

Marketing Situation

The hosiery market in the United States consists of two parts: the high end and "all other." The high end is dominated by a few national brands. Private labels constitute the remainder of the market. Technological improvement in both yarn and knitting mill machinery have minimized the distinctive product superiority of any one brand. Finding a new feature with distinct advantages became the goal of a leading manufacturer who wanted to regain the brand franchise previously enjoyed. Such a feature was recognized in a new product development which offered the therapeutic benefits of a surgical stocking and the sheer beauty of conventional dress hose.

Advertising had a distinct job to do:

1. Make people aware of the brand name (for purposes of illustration we shall call the brand "Therabeautic").

2. Convey the messages that:

   a) "Therabeautic" offers the support of a surgical stocking with the beauty of dress hose.

   b) "Therabeautic" is not just for consumers with varicose veins who require such hose for medical reasons, but for all active people who must be on their feet a lot. Thus, it is an "antifatigue" stocking.

   c) "Therabeautic" is economical. While the cost per pair is high, this stocking will outwear several pairs of conventional nylon hose.

Advertising was given the task of conveying these messages so convincingly that consumers would ask retailers for "Therabeautic," and thus aid in getting more widespread distribution.

Measurement

The product was introduced in selected key markets. A heavy local schedule was essential to persuade a nucleus of leading retailers (who know the value of advertising) to stock the line. Because retailers are quite sensitive to customer requests for products not in stock, advertising must do the job of stimulating customer requests to encourage retailers to stock the product.

A simple research method was used to supplement the normal process of gauging advertising effectiveness by means of current sales and inquiries. Interviewers were stationed in selected department stores near the hosiery department. With the cooperation of the sales staff, customers who bought, inquired about, or examined the product, were asked a few simple questions. (How did they learn about the product? What appealed to them, etc.?) At other locations in the store, a cross section of customers was surveyed on the simple question of brand awareness.

Through this process, it was learned that over 50% of the purchases and inquiries were stimulated by advertising (the balance came from recommendation, display, and other sources).

Once the product was established, the weight of advertising effort (which needed to be abnormally heavy for launching and acquiring distribution) was reduced to a normal level. Corporate advertising went to national and spot media, while dealer cooperative advertising continued in strictly local media.

Consumer research uncovered the need for a shift of copy emphasis after the product was established. Consumers were happy with the comfort feature, but tended to resist repeat purchases because of price. Advertising concentrated more heavily on the economy theme. Consumer attitude studies were conducted on a continuing basis to determine the effectiveness of communicating the key advertising messages. The following example concerns electrical appliances but serves to illustrate other consumer durables as well, such as automobiles or furniture.

Example 7: Electrical Appliances

Background

Market: 75 million logical prospects among homemakers

Marketing Goal: Reduce excess year-end dealer inventories to normal level

Advertising Goal: Persuade 400,000 homemakers to visit 20,000 dealers in four weeks

---

Marketing Situation

The market is 75 million homemakers who are logical prospects. Logical prospects are defined as those whose appliances are at least three years old, plus new households formed by marriage and new home construction.

Marketing Objective

Get sales action now, sell carloads of appliances this season, thus reducing substantial dealer and manufacturer inventories.

Advertising Objective

Induce immediate action. Specifically, persuade homemakers to visit dealers' showrooms and see a demonstration. A special premium is offered as an added incentive. The brand name and product advantages are already well known through consistent and effective advertising.

Specific Advertising Goal

To persuade 400,000 homemakers to visit 20,000 dealers in four weeks—an average of 20 prospects physically crossing the threshold of each dealer's showroom.

Two TV specials drew a combined audience of 84 million people. Approximately 18%, or 15 million people, could play back the commercial messages, which also offered premiums. Nearly a half million persons took immediate action by walking into a dealer's showroom and obtaining the premium. Advertising then, accomplished its assigned task by inducing consumers to visit the dealer's showroom, where the sales personnel took over to sell the appliances, deal with trade-ins, credit, etc. Dealers sold an increased volume of appliances during the special promotion.

Example 8: Building Materials

Background

Market:	125,000 architects
	625,000 builders
	31,000,000 prospective purchasers of single-family dwellings
Marketing Goal:	Increase share of residential insulation industry from 10% to 14% in three years
Advertising Goals:	• Register all-round economy message with 40% of architects
	• Register speed of installation message with 30% of builders
	• Attain 50% brand identity among prospective owners

The subject company manufactures a line of building materials used in residential and commercial construction. One of the principal items is insulation. The company employs over 100 salespeople who sell through distributors and also directly to builders, architects and, in some cases, owners.

Marketing Situation

Advertising has been used for many years with generally favorable reactions as to its effectiveness. In recent years there has been increased demand on the part of management for better evidence of the results of advertising. No questions were raised about the value of sales promotion materials, such as spec. sheets and catalogs. There was some division of opinion, however, on the cost benefits for two categories of advertising:

- *Trade paper advertising to architects and builders*
- *Consumer advertising to homeowners.*

A measurement program was undertaken to get better answers to this question. This required, first, a definition of what the company wanted to accomplish through advertising. The ultimate objective is to sell insulation (and other products) at a profit but, in order to do this, certain messages must be conveyed to certain markets.

The first market is the architect. The job is to get the architect to specify the company's brand of insulation.

The second market is the builder. There are two jobs to be done here: First, to get the builder's favorable reaction when the architect specifies or the owner mentions the product; second, to get the builder to select these materials for houses built on speculation. Low installation cost is the builder's primary motive.

The third market is the owner. Very few owners specify the brand of insulation. The objective is to get owners to recognize the brand name, to associate the name with fuel economy, and to react favorably when the architect or builder mentions the brand.

The following is the size of market, the message, and the three-year advertising goals for each:

1. Architects

   Size of market: 125,000 architects

   Message: Best all-round economy (savings in initial cost of heating system and fuel costs more than offset added insulation costs)

   Goal: Register message with 40% of architects.

2. Builders

   Size of market: 625,000 residential builders

   Message: Speed of installation and all-round economy on "spec-built" houses

   Goal: Register message with 30% of builders.

3. Owners

   Size of market: 3,000,000 prospective owners of single-family dwelling units

   Message: Savings in fuel bills

   Goals: 50% brand name recognition

        25% who associate brand name with fuel savings.

Example 9: Local Brand of Beer

Background

Market:	500,000 moderate to heavy beer drinkers in urban area recently entered by the brand
Marketing Goal:	Capture 8% share of market in two years
Advertising Goal:	Attain 80% brand recognition within six months after introduction

This brand of beer has been the largest-selling brand in its headquarter's market for generations. The company has gradually expanded distribution into contiguous markets and now distributes in over a dozen states.

Company Policy

Avoid entering a new market until ready to go all out on advertising and distribution. The first year in a new market, advertising expense, as a percent of sales, will run three or four times the normal expenditure in an established market. It may take two or three years to reach the break-even point.

When first entering a new market, brand awareness is low. It is necessary to match or outspend the largest selling brand in order to capture a share of consumers' attention and gradually woo them to try the brand. Management believes that anyone who is not prepared to enter competitive combat, quantitatively and qualitatively, is wasting their money trying to open up new markets in this industry.

Advertising Objective

Deep and incessant exposure. The goal is to establish an 80% level of brand recognition among moderate-to-heavy beer drinkers in the market area within sixth months and to maintain that level thereafter. Through a series of simple unaided and aided recall tests, consumers are asked to identify various brands of beer sold and advertised in the market area. Experience in past market introductions has shown that the brand has always succeeded in getting a firm foothold in a market where an 80% brand awareness level has been established. Once the brand name is established through "investment" advertising, expenditures, as a percentage of the sales dollar, return to a normal level.

Example 10: Special Steel Rolled Bar Sections

Background

Market:	189,000 design and production personnel in machining departments and shops using rolled steel bars
Marketing Situation:	Low level of awareness of product type, and low comprehension of product benefits
Marketing Goal:	Average annual tonnage increase of 8% over next five years
Advertising Goal:	Communicate cost- and time-saving advantages of product to one-fourth of buying influencers in one year

---

The company manufactures a broad line of steel products used in hundreds of different industries for fabricating thousands of different products made of steel.

Past advertising had been successful. It had helped build the company's reputation for quality products and for technical capabilities in producing large and intricate steel products. However, customers tend to think of the company in terms of the more glamorous applications such as huge turbine motors, atomic energy and missile applications. Advertising emphasis on technical capability in such applications had overshadowed the more prosaic products applications that account for the great bulk of sales and profit dollars. For example:

- Only a small percentage of forged products users interviewed were aware that the company makes forged rolls and sleeves.

- The advertising had failed to communicate the time and cost advantages of special rolled bar sections to machine designers and machine shop operators.

- A disturbingly large percentage of the customer audience was not aware that the company is a major supplier of coal-tar chemicals.

The advertising had been successful in communicating an image of the company's advanced technology, quality, application, and know-how. But the time had come for more concrete advertising objectives:

- To increase customer awareness of specific products and applications.
- To increase comprehension of the specific advantages and benefits of these products in terms of familiar customer applications.

In brief, a shift was made in advertising philosophy and policy—from broad "image" or "umbrella" type advertising to specific product feature and advantage advertising. The shift was needed, not because past advertising had been ineffective; on the contrary, it had done its job so well that only a "maintenance level" of image type advertising would be required in the future. Hence, major emphasis was shifted to communicating information about the advantages of specific products.

This change in policy required a complete inventory of the status of customer knowledge and attitude for each product category and industry application. The "CUSTOMER KNOWLEDGE AND ATTITUDE INVENTORY" included these steps:

1. Determine the number of "buying influencers" for each product application. For example, the study determined the total number of people influential in the buying and specifying of steel forgings used in the automotive industry, high-strength steel used by manufacturers of pressure vessels, structural steel used in bridges and dozens of similar industry applications. These "buying influencers" were further classified by title (design engineer, superintendent, purchasing agent, etc.).

2. The next step was to determine the level of knowledge and attitude of these buying influencers:

a) Awareness of the existence of the product (or awareness that the company makes the product).

b) Understanding of the chief advantages, benefits, and applications of the product.

c) Attitude toward purchase (degree of favorable or unfavorable attitude).

This kind of information about customers, their state of knowledge and attitude, had not previously been available. In fact, existing data provided no more than sales by type and size of customer. Information on the number and title of *individuals* within the customer organization who influenced purchases and the state of their knowledge and attitude regarding products were unheard of.

Yet such information was essential in order to set advertising goals, design messages, select media and, finally, to measure accomplishment.

Obviously, this represented a large and costly information-gathering job. Hence, it was decided to restrict the first year's effort to a single product line or industry in each of several broad categories. An example of such a product line is special rolled bar sections. The advertising goals set up for this product line were as follows:

1. To communicate to product designers the cost and time savings in using special sections rolled to the approximate contour of the finished item, rather than machining the parts from regular round or square bars.

2. To illustrate their superior strength and impact resistance compared with castings.

Advertising was designed to convey these specific messages to a designated audience. Before the advertising ran, a "benchmark" survey was conducted to determine the present state of knowledge. Measured advertising goals were then set for the coming year on the variables indicated below.

A second survey, using comparable methodology, was conducted after the campaign had run for one year. The following results illustrate the process (although figures are fictitious).

	Pre-Advertising Survey	Post-Advertising Survey
Aware of the product type (special rolled sections)	55%	80%
Identified name of manufacturer	30%	58%
Could play back advantages:		
a) Time and cost saving	8%	27%
b) Greater strength, impact resistance	14%	21%
Favorable attitude toward purchase	10%	18%

Because the total advertising expenditure was small, a costly research project was not warranted. The two surveys were conducted by mail, with supplemental personal interviews conducted among a sample of respondents. The cost of the two research studies was modest in relation to the improved advertising impact through concentrating on well-defined objectives.

Example 11: Corporate Image

Background

Overall
Communications
Objectives: Increase corporate identity and favorable
attitude among:

- Shareholders and potential investors
- Industrial goods customers and prospects
- Consumer goods customers and prospects
- Employees and potential employees
- Retailers, distributors, and suppliers
- Local, state, and federal government
  (procurement, legislative and regulatory
  agencies)

Advertising Goal: Increase overall level of knowledge and
favorable attitude by an average of 5%
annually for five years

The Corporate Communications Problem

The Corporation is composed of many divisions that manufacture a broad line of industrial and consumer goods. Extensive laboratory research and product development programs have resulted in a stream of new products entering the market each year. Last year, 40% of the Corporation's revenue and over 60% of the net profit came from products that were not on the market 10 years ago.

This poses a number of problems in the area of corporate identification, product identification, and relationships with various sectors of the public.

1. Today the Corporation is selling to industries far removed from the basic industry upon which the

---

business was founded. Industrial salespeople find it more difficult to gain entry, acceptance and confidence in these industries than in those where the Corporation is traditionally well known.

2. Association of branded consumer goods with the corporate name is relatively low among consumers, retailers and distributors.

3. In addition, the wide diversity of products and services creates confusion in the minds of other sectors of the public including:

   • Investor public personnel (financial professionals, shareholders and potential share holders)

   • Government (military procurement, government works, legislative)

   • General public (employees, potential employees, customers, distributors, suppliers, etc.).

There was some dissension among executive, sales, advertising and public relations personnel as to the value of so-called "corporate image" advertising. Some felt advertising money was better spent in selling specific products to specific markets and industries. Others thought there were economies and advantages in selling on a united corporate front. The division of opinion varied between those at one extreme who wanted to abolish all corporate advertising and spend the money on direct product advertising and, at the opposite extreme, those who felt that product advertising is most effective when backed by a strong corporate campaign.

Measurement Program

A measurement program was directed toward getting better answers to these questions:

   • How effective is corporate advertising in making the Corporation well known and well regarded among specific segments of the public?

- To what extent does being "well known" and "well regarded" actually contribute to the profitable sale of products and to other corporate objectives?

Management did not expect to get "hard and fast" answers to these questions, but the following measurement program placed management in a position to make much sounder judgment.

It was realized, in embarking upon a measurement program, that there was no clear understanding by management or the agency on the question: "What kind of image does the Corporation want to communicate?" It would obviously be difficult and perhaps misleading to measure accomplishment without first knowing the information and mental attitude to be conveyed to various segments of the public.

The problem—defining corporate communications objectives—proved to be far more difficult and time consuming than imagined. It required an audit of the public's attitudes to find out:

- *How well known is the Corporation at the present time?*
- *What is it known for?*
- *Scale of attitudes*
- *Sources of information or attitude.*

It was decided to determine the above information for each segment of the total audience (such as customers, potential customers, employees, investors, government procurement agencies, etc.).

Relative Influence

The study further identified the relative "buying influence" of people in each segment of the public. For example, it showed the relative influence of purchasing agents, engineers, and treasurers in each major industry to which industrial products are sold and, in a similar way, the influence of various people in such segments of the public as personnel recruitment and government procurement.

How Large Is the Market?

For the first time in the Corporation's advertising history, attention was focused on determining the size of each audience segment. Partly through research, and partly through experience and judgment, a considered estimate was made of the number of "buying influencers" in each market or public segment.

For example, about 8% of the Corporation's sales go to the automotive industry. The argument has been advanced in the past that with only a half dozen large customers in this industry, why advertise? However, size-of-audience research indicated that 11,500 people have a direct influence on the specification and purchase of products in this one industry alone. In government procurement, it had been erroneously assumed that a few people sitting around the Pentagon were the ones to be informed and sold. The number of "influentials" turned out to be in the magnitude of 25,000. Similar figures were arrived at for dozens of other public and market segments.

Summary of Present Image

The public attitude study brought out these key points:

- The Corporation is not as well known as management would like it to be, particularly among certain key groups.
- The general image of the Corporation is somewhat confused, not particularly favorable and at least 20 years behind the times. A large segment of the

people, including many important buying influencers, have outdated mental images of products, facilities and practice.

Has Past Corporate Advertising Been Ineffective?

The research and internal soul-searching brought up another consideration. Sizable sums have been spent for several years on corporate advertising. Does this mean that corporate image advertising, per se, is ineffective and should be dispensed with?

Before jumping to this conclusion, past corporate advertising efforts were impartially reviewed and these conclusions were drawn:

- Past advertising efforts lacked any central, consistent aim or theme. It could hardly have been otherwise, since management had not previously consolidated its communication objectives and policies.

- The advertising was strongly self-oriented and not customer-benefit-oriented, with consequent low readership and remembrance factors.

Ineffectiveness of past communications pointed, not to advertising as a medium, but to failure to define clearly what kind of an image the Corporation wanted to communicate, and to what particular audience.

What Kind of an Image Needs to Be Communicated?

With this foundation of the size and character of the audience, and the knowledge of and attitude toward the Corporation, the next step was to explore the question, "What kind of image does the Corporation want to build?"

Communication Objectives

These were first broadly defined as follows: to increase knowledge and favorable attitude toward the Corporation among certain defined segments of the public on the following points:

- Technological and scientific leadership
- Dynamic growth corporation
- Quality of products (achieved through rigid testing, quality control, modern facilities, training, and skill of personnel)
- Superior, nationwide technical service facilities
- Corporate citizenship (including such factors as employee esprit de corps and benefits, contribution to national well-being, environmental concerns, community and interbusiness relationships).

Arriving at these broad communication objectives required the full participation of management at the policy-making level (failure to clarify these views responsible for past limited effectiveness of corporate advertising).

In examining the data on the current corporate image, it was discovered that the Corporation rated higher on the above points among the "well-informed" than among the "poorly-informed." For example, on the point of technological and scientific leadership, the well-informed group rated the Corporation twice as high as did the poorly-informed group. This merely confirmed the truism, "Those who know you well are more inclined to regard you favorably." Clearly, the problem was to enlarge, through advertising, the size of the well-informed group.

Advertising Goals

Public attitude studies showed that the present level of knowledge and favorable attitude toward the Corporation was 22% (last item in table below):

	Present Level
Technical and scientific leadership	20%
Dynamic growth corporation	15%
Quality of products	18%
Technical service facilities	8%
Corporate citizenship	9%
Overall knowledge and favorable attitude	22%

A specific goal was set up to increase overall knowledge and favorable attitude an average of 5% annually for five years. Hence, at the end of five years the goal would be achieved if the corporation's identity-favorability index increased from 22% to 47%.

Agency's Responsibility

The advertising agency participated throughout the entire goal definition process. The understanding with the agency was briefly as follows: It is the advertiser's job to decide *what* to communicate. It is the agency's job to determine *how* best to communicate; to recommend the kind of copy, the media, and the volume of advertising required to reach the goals. The agency is expected to support its recommendations with facts, experience and logic. If the cost is excessive, the Corporation will scale down its goals and establish a priority of importance. If first-year goals are exceeded, this is evidence of the power of well-directed advertising. New and higher goals might then be considered.

Example 12: Portable Electronic Test Equipment

Background

Market: 400,000 managerial, technical, and operating personnel in airframe, airline, and electronic systems companies

Marketing Goal: Sell or lease test equipment to 25% of potential users

Advertising Goal: Increase penetration of message, "More operational aircraft hours," from 15% to 50% in two years

---

The company manufactures electronic equipment for testing instruments and components of aircraft. Because this is a completely integrated and portable system, it is possible to test aircraft as a normal operating procedure; it is not necessary to take the aircraft "to the laboratory"—the laboratory, instead, is taken to the aircraft. Hence, the system results in a 30% increase in operational aircraft hours.

Marketing Situation

The market has been estimated as 400,000 officials and technical and operating personnel in airframe, airline and electronic systems companies. These are the people who must be convinced of the advantages of Portable Electronic Test Equipment.

Channels available for communicating with the market include the company's sales force, advertising, literature, news stories in technical journals, and trade shows. All of these channels provide information and stimulate discussion among engineering, operating and management personnel.

After thorough consideration, it was decided that the major task of advertising was to concentrate on one key message—the substantial savings in operational aircraft hours.

A survey of buying influences in prospective customer organizations showed the following:

Acquainted with the product type	75%
Correctly identified the manufacturer	55%
Can play back the key message (Portable Electronic Test Equipment makes possible a 30% increase in operational aircraft hours)	15%

Advertising Goal

To increase comprehension of this key message among the target audience from 15% to 50% in two years. Results are measured by repeating the survey of buying influences annually.

Example 13: Pain Reliever

Background	
Market:	Entire adult population
Marketing Goals:	Maintain present share of headache remedy market
	Increase share of cold relief market from 8% to 12% in three years
Advertising Goals:	Hold present level of message penetration on headache relief (35% level)
	Increase cold relief message penetration from 15% to 25% in six months

The manufacturer of a leading brand of pain reliever has been advertising for years that this brand gives "fast relief." Leading competitors have also made this claim the central theme of their advertising. At the present time, the three leading brands have the following rankings in public awareness and attitude (as determined by consumer surveys):

	Brand *A*	Brand *B*	Brand *C*
Brand awareness:			
(Answers to the question: "What brands of headache remedies and pain relievers can you name?")	87	78	69
Message registration:			
(Answers to the question: "Which of these brands do you associate with fast relief?")	36	38	41

For some time, the three leading brands have remained just about equal on this claim of fast relief, according to periodic surveys. In other words, the competitive situation is virtually at a standstill on this particular product benefit and claim.

Advertising Strategy for Brand *A*

After careful study of market data, the following has been decided:

> Physicians widely recommended this general product type for colds. Wider use of the product for colds offers the largest opportunity for increased sales. At the same time, it is necessary to maintain a high standing in the public mind on the claim, "fast relief for headaches." The company has a large advertising investment in this claim and does not intend to abandon it to competitors. ■

Hence the strategy:

- *Maintain* present position on "fast relief"
- *Advance* in penetration of message, "at the first sign of a cold, take two tablets of Brand A."

During seasons when the danger of colds is high, the cold relief theme gets major treatment; headache theme, minor treatment. At all other times, the speedy headache relief theme is foremost. This strategy was launched in test markets where the company maintains both store audits, showing actual sale of goods week-by-week, and consumer panels, showing consumption of the product (via medicine cabinet inventory and consumer purchase diaries). Results in the test markets were as follows:

	Beginning of Test Period	End of Test Period
Headache message registration	36%	34%
Cold relief message registration	15%	28%

Over the years it was found that message registration definitely results in increased sale of the products. However, there is considerable lag effect. This lag effect is caused by several factors:

1. Consumers who get the message and decide to use the product often have a considerable inventory on hand. This is especially true since the company has successfully promoted the large family-size package in recent years.

2. There may be a period of several weeks or months between the time of the "message registration" and the occasion which calls for use of the product (cold or headache).

3. Even the weather can have an effect. A "ward-off-colds" message which coincides with a spell of bad weather can be reflected more quickly in sales than the same message delivered during a period of fair weather.

Hence, it is misleading to judge the success of the advertising strictly on the basis of short-term sales activity. It is more reliable to measure advertising in terms of message registration and then relate message registration to long-term consumption and sales results.

Example 14: Regional Brand of Gasoline

Background

Market:	18 million motorists in 14 states
Marketing Goal:	Halt competitive inroads into share of market
Advertising Goals:	• Increase the awareness level of the existence of beneficial chemical additives in gasoline from 50% to 75%
	• Establish among at least three-quarters of the motorists that Brand *A* is the leading brand in searching for and providing benefits for its users

---

This case history concerns a regional brand of gasoline. The company was faced with the threat of a declining share of market caused by new competitors entering the geographic area in which the company has historically held a strong position. The company's marketing management recognized that the first step toward more effective advertising was for company management and advertising agency personnel to see eye-to-eye on *the purpose and function of advertising in the company.* Hence a series of meetings was held in which sales, research, marketing and general management people of the advertiser company met with various people in the agency to discuss and evolve both an advertising "philosophy" and an advertising "strategy."

"No holds barred" discussions between these groups raised the following issues:

- What advertising can, and cannot be expected to do in our business.
- Why do we advertise—what do we seek to accomplish through advertising?
- Complete analysis of products and services, perceived and actual: Where do we suffer competitive disadvantages? Where are we on a par with competition on the points of product and service superiority?

For the first time, as a result of these meetings, the advertising, sales, technical, and financial people began to see eye-to-eye on the true purpose and capabilities of advertising. In previous years, the advertising team had developed an annual "pitch" or budget presentation complete with copy and media recommendations. In the new approach, discussions were held many months in advance of the budget and copy approval period. The agenda was restricted to discussion of the question: *What* do we have to communicate? Techniques of *how* to communicate (media, copy) were off limits at these "think" sessions.

The conclusions reached in the area of marketing communication objectives were briefly as follows:

Broad Marketing Objectives

1. Bring new customers into the company stations
2. Make steady customers out of occasional users
3. Hold present users against competition

4. Increase ratio of premium grade sales to regular grade sales

5. Increase the sale of oil, tires, batteries and accessories to present customers

6. Enlarge the entire market by encouraging tourism in the area.

Advertising is one of several forces that help accomplish these broad marketing objectives. Other forces include the stations themselves (number, location, design, signing, cleanliness, etc.), the attitude and training of station attendants, the quality of products, product packaging and display, price, etc.

Advertising can contribute to all of the above marketing objectives. However, if the same ad or campaign tries to do all of these things, it is not likely to succeed to a measurable extent in any one of them.

Advertising's Function

Management of the company and agency jointly concluded that the primary purpose and role of advertising is as follows:

Advertising aims primarily at getting new customers and retaining the old with concentration on the spearhead of the product line—gasoline. Advertising is seldom capable of bringing about an immediate "brand switch." This is true because big and dramatic product superiority features do not come along very often in this industry and motorists' gasoline-purchasing routines are difficult to change. ■

However, Brand A *does* have certain superior features and advantages over leading competitive makes.

Contrary to popular misconceptions, all leading brands of gasoline are *not* alike. Discussions between the company's research and development people and those responsible for advertising resulted in the following product information:

> All brands of gasoline used on the highways (farm and marine uses are excluded) contain "chemical additives." ∎

Brand *A* contains seven principal additives:

1. *Anti-Oxidant* (keeps gasoline from going "bad" or "stale" while in storage)
2. *Metal Deactivator* (prevents copper from acting as a catalyst to form gum)

    (Items 1 and 2 above are additives the company provides to insure top quality gasoline *before* it gets into the motorist's tank. The remaining additives provide benefits after purchase by the motorist.)

3. *Corrosion Inhibitor* (prevents rust)
4. *Detergent* (cleans carburetor and fuel systems)
5. *Anti-icing Agent* (prevents ice from building up in carburetor during certain conditions of temperature and humidity)
6. *Antiknock Compound* (reduces "ping" caused by pre-ignition)
7. *Phosphorus* (modifies deposits).

Consumer research showed that, with the exception of the antiknock compound, motorists were almost completely unaware of the extra benefits built into the fuel. Furthermore, research indicated that many motorists believe that all brands of gas are more or less alike. It is true that 99% of all gasolines contain antiknock compounds. However, there are some important differences beyond this.

For example, only about 50% of the gasoline sold contains phosphorus. This means nothing to motorists until they understand what it does for them. Phosphorus prevents spark-plug fouling, pre-ignition of fuel (which results in engine "knocking") and loss of full power and efficiency.

Only about 25% of the gasoline pumped contains detergent. A detergent prevents "gunk" from forming in the carburetor and changing the fuel-air ratio. This results in hard starting, stalling, and again, in loss of engine efficiency.

What Is Expected?

Conclusions reached on the job of advertising were, briefly, as follows: Advertising's job is to communicate to motorists the differences and benefits which *we* know about, but which the *motoring public* is unaware of.

Advertising's job is to get these differences and benefits across in simple language and illustration. Motorists don't know or care what phosphorus is, but they understand the difference between a clean spark plug and one that is all fouled up. Just as homemakers know what a detergent is, they are acutely aware of a car that is hard to start or one that stalls at the wrong time with everybody honking at them and giving them dirty looks. Advertising's job is to provide a link between the familiar and unfamiliar. The consumers don't know or care about anti-oxidant, but they do understand the analogy with stale eggs or bad breath. Advertising's job is more than communicating these "differences." Its job is to create (through repetitive examples) a *frame of mind regarding the company and brand.* Advertising's job is to build *confidence* that the company is constantly on the alert, behind the scenes, to improve the product to the benefit of motorists.

Translating "Philosophy" into Defined Goals and Measured Results

The above "philosophy" or area of understanding on what was expected of advertising needed to be translated into hard, measurable criteria. The conclusion was reached that advertising effectiveness would be judged on its accomplishment of two tasks:

1. The number of motorists who are *aware* of the differences between Brand *A* gasoline and competing brands and of the benefits that Brand *A* brings.
2. The number of motorists who consider Brand *A* superior or outstanding in searching for and providing benefits to the consumer.

In order to make these goals specific and measurable, it was necessary to conduct research among a representative sample of the motoring public in the marketing area. The first research study was conducted to establish a benchmark and set measurable advertising goals. Later studies were conducted to determine progress in communicating "the intended messages to the intended audiences." The following survey results, while not actual data, are illustrative of the process:

	Benchmark Survey (Before Advertising)	Progress Report (After Advertising)
Awareness of differences between Brand *A* and competing brands	5%	32%
Consider Brand *A* superior or outstanding in developing and providing consumer benefits	12%	42%

Without endeavoring to specify the precise research techniques used, the following is indicative: A representative probability sample of motorists was selected. Prior to the advertising campaign, and at six-month intervals thereafter, questions similar to the following were asked of successive independently selected samples.

1. "No doubt you have used or read about several different brands of gasoline. Can you think of any ways in which the gasoline of one manufacturer is different from that of another?"

   Answers were coded according to whether messages contained in the ads had registered with the consumer. For example, the following verbatim answer was credited as message registration: "They put stuff in the gas that keeps the carburetor and gas lines clean."

2. "Here are five cards containing the names of brands of gasoline sold in this area. Please tell me what brand you think is doing the best job of providing the motorist with improved gasoline." (Consumers were further queried until brands were marked 1 to 5).

Further analysis of survey results on the basis of brand switching and brand loyalty enabled the evaluation of advertising results in terms of new customer acquisition and old customer retention. This further enabled management to make calculated estimates of long-range sales and profits attributable to advertising.

Example 15: Ethical Drug Product

Background

Market:	350,000 office-based doctors
Marketing Goal:	Establish position and reputation as the leading producer in this category of drug products
Advertising Goals:	• Inform 50% of doctors about improved formula in two years
	• Convince 25% that it is safe and effective for hypertension

---

This example concerns a product in the ethical drug field: meprobamate, popularly known as a "tranquilizer."

Market

Market consists of 350,000 office-based doctors. Key factor in the marketing situation is an improved product made possible by adding meprobamate to a diuretic.

Advertising Goals

- First, to inform 50%, or 175,000 doctors, within three months, of the improved product which virtually eliminates undesirable side effects.

- Second, to convince 25%, or about 90,000 doctors, that the product is safe, effective and a significant advance as a drug indicated for hypertension.

Measurement of results was accomplished through research among a panel of doctors who periodically answered questions regarding knowledge and specification of ethical drug products.

The research study further identified sources of information about drug products to which the doctors have been exposed, such as:

A—Advertising in medical journals

B—Direct mail literature

C—News stories and articles in medical journals

D—Calls by "detail people"

E—Discussions with other medical people

Stringent research methods were employed to verify sources of information. For reasons of simplicity, findings are shown only for items A (advertising) and D (detail people):

	Awareness (Familiar with name of brand and manufacturer)	Conviction (Favorably disposed toward prescribing product for certain conditions)
A (not D)	38%	14%
D (not A)	30%	18%
Neither A nor D	12%	10%
Both A and D	56%	28%

The above figures show that advertising is effective in creating awareness and favorable attitude among those doctors who were *not* contacted by detail people. But, most important, the combination of a personal call plus advertising resulted in a high degree of awareness and conviction. These data enable management to evaluate costs and results for advertising as well as other forms of marketing communication.

The results indicated that advertising is an efficient way to get information about product improvements, benefits, and limitations to the medical profession, and, thus, aid doctors in prescribing for their patients. The practice of using detail people to make personal calls on doctors was recognized as a costly but essential function. Advertising could not entirely perform certain functions, which require personal contact of technically informed people. But advertising can supplement detail people, reduce their communicating workload, and thus contribute toward an overall reduction in distribution costs in the drug industry.

Example 16: Cranberries

Background	
Market:	People who prepare food at home
Marketing Goal:	Increase sale of cranberries through new and diversified uses
Advertising Goals:	Achieve following in one year:

• Heard about cranberry bread	50%
• Would like to bake it	25%
• Have baked it	10%

Marketing Situation

The hypothetical trade association is made up of growers of cranberries including many small producers who cannot afford to advertise individually. Consumption of cranberries is highly seasonal, traditionally peaking during the Thanksgiving and Christmas seasons. A poor season, because of weather or other conditions, threatens to wipe out many producers who depend upon this single crop for their livelihood. The land is unsuitable for crop diversification. Hence, the salvation of many growers lies in better marketing. Broad marketing objectives are:

1. Increase consumption of cranberries

2. Diversify use of cranberries so that marketing activities are not crowded into one short season.

Marketing Strategy

Develop new uses of the product and create consumer demand through advertising, publicity, and promotion. The first step was to engage food technologists and home economists to develop delectable new recipes. Result: An exciting new product, cranberry bread, was developed and tested.

Advertising Goals

To spread the word among homemakers that cranberry bread is delicious, easy to bake, and a culinary accomplishment that will bring praise to the cook by all who taste it. Specifically, these one-year goals were set:

Awareness (have heard about cranberry bread)	50% of market
Favorable attitude (would like to bake it)	25% of market
Action (have baked it)	10% of market

Since the advertising funds of cranberry growers were very limited, it was necessary to get participation and tie-in advertising of others who would benefit, such as flour millers, nut growers, etc. With advertising as the pivotal force, retailers were willing to devote display space, food editors treated the new items editorially, and manufacturers of flour and other products were persuaded to include recipes on packages.

Measurements of Results

Proof of advertising performance was needed to convince all of the cooperating groups of the success of the initial effort and of the advantages of continued support. The sales volume of cranberries was not, by itself, a suitable index of the advertising effectiveness. The entire crop is always disposed of, if necessary, at distress prices. Furthermore, the price received is also not a reliable index, since abundance of crops is governed by weather and other factors. Hence, measurement of the effectiveness of advertising alone was needed. This measurement was accomplished through a consumer panel survey to determine the percentage of homemakers who had heard about, wanted to try, or had actually baked the product. Results clearly indicated the success of the first year's campaign and the desirability of continued promotional efforts, with emphasis on converting those who know about the product to repetitive users.

Example 17: Home Computers

Background

Market: Upper and middle income families with school age children

Marketing Goal: Sell 400,000 units of company's brand of PC computers within the next 12 months

Advertising Goals: • Create "reliability" as an important consideration in the selection of a brand to be purchased by at least 80% of the market

• Raise the awareness of the existence of its local service facilities among potential purchasers from 5% to 60%

Marketing Strategy

The use of a computer is becoming an integral part of a child's education. According to the U.S. Department of Education, 29 percent of all students used computers in school in 1984. In 1988, the figure had risen to 46 percent. Students whose family income is in the top quarter nationally are more than twice as likely to use a computer at school as those in the lowest quarter. Practically every school has a computer available to students, the number ranging from one for every student to one for every 20 students. The latter ratio does not allow students sufficient practice to enhance their skills.

A national survey of upper income parents indicated that they felt students with a computer at home can become proficient in its use and find it helpful in preparing assignments. However, many expressed misgivings about purchasing one. A large portion of these parents do not know how to use computers and many fear that they would not know what to do if the computer jams.

On the basis of this survey, it was recommended that computer manufacturers provide instructions to parents either in the form of written documents or a short course. An emergency phone number should be given to the purchaser so that immediate attention can be given to any problem that may arise.

Advertising Strategy

An advertising campaign in a number of family and parent magazines was undertaken to emphasize the advantages that can accrue when a student has a computer at home: it would help the student in school work, encourage the child's desire for learning, and be useful to parents.

The advertising gave a toll-free number to call for more information and also a coupon for a request for a special brochure.

Measurement

The results of the campaign were also measured by the number of telephone calls received, the number of requests, and a follow-up survey among the same target group.

Example 18: Casual Slacks

	Background
Market:	People 25 to 50 years of age who shop for casual slacks
Marketing Goal:	Increase the sales of the brand's slacks in department stores
Advertising Goal:	Raise the perception of the quality of the brand being "excellent" or "good" from 65% to 85% among shoppers who are "aware of the brand"

For a number of years, this national brand of slacks had been successfully marketed in discount clothing stores. The brand became very popular among teenagers who wore them for sports, at discos, and just for "hanging around." As the population aged, the company decided to take advantage of its success among former teenagers, upgrade the product, and market the slacks in department stores. However, the sales in this market did not do very well.

In a group of test markets where there were four national and a number of private label brands, the advertiser's brand was among its three national competitors in terms of high brand awareness. Among the four, the perceptions of high quality and good styling were the lowest for the advertiser's brand. These findings were confirmed in a nationwide study.

Physical tests for quality showed no differences among this and the other national brands. The slacks were restyled. The company then instituted an advertising campaign in fashion, leisure, and news magazines. The copy showed men and women in different outdoor situations wearing these slacks.

As a result of the campaign, the ratings for both styling and quality increased. During the following spring season, there was a marked increase in the advertiser's brand share.

Example 19: Replacement Radial Tires

Background	
Market:	The 20 million passenger-car owners in the United States who purchase one or more radial tires in a six-month period
Marketing Situation:	A highly competitive market with about 50 brands available
Marketing Goal:	Increase the current market share of less than 10% to 15%
Advertising Goals:	• Increase the awareness of the company as a maker of radial tires from 20% to 50% within a six-month period
	• Communicate that its tires are longer lasting

This tire company has been in business for a number of years. Its main source of business was the automobile manufacturers who used this brand of tires as original equipment. Its share of sales in the replacement market has never been too high—ranging from 8% to 10%. While most motorists were familiar with the brand, less than 20% knew that the company sold radial tires.

Marketing Strategy

The market consists of two parts. One part consists of young "hot rods" whose concern is with performance under adverse conditions such as short stops and fast cornering as well as fast acceleration and deceleration. The other part consists of conservative drivers whose main concerns are with comfort and safety under normal driving conditions. This group tends to be older and to keep a car longer than the other group. Because of its reputation and history, the company decided to concentrate on the second part.

Advertising Strategy

A nationwide survey indicated that (1) the awareness of this company as a maker of radial tires was 20%, (2) the advantages of radial tires in terms of safety and comfort was recognized as a generic characteristic, (3) long lasting was not an issue among younger motorists, but was important to older prospects. The initial advertising approach was designed to make prospects aware that the company made radial tires and that its tires were longer lasting.

TITLES OF INTEREST IN
ADVERTISING, SALES PROMOTION, AND PUBLIC RELATIONS

CUSTOMER BONDING, by Richard Cross and Janet Smith

INTEGRATED MARKETING COMMUNICATIONS, by Don E. Schultz, Stanley I. Tannenbaum, and Robert F. Lauterborn

PROMOTIONAL MARKETING, by William A. Robinson and Christine Hauri

SALES PROMOTION ESSENTIALS, by Don E. Schultz, William A. Robinson, and Lisa A.Petrison

SALES PROMOTION MANAGEMENT, by Don E. Schultz and William A. Robinson

BEST SALES PROMOTIONS, by William A. Robinson

SUCCESSFUL DIRECT MARKETING METHODS, by Bob Stone

CREATIVE STRATEGY IN DIRECT MARKETING, by Susan K. Jones

PROFITABLE DIRECT MARKETING, by Jim Kobs

INTEGRATED DIRECT MARKETING, by Ernan Roman

COMMONSENSE DIRECT MARKETING, by Drayton Bird

BEYOND 2000: THE FUTURE OF DIRECT MARKETING, by Jerry I. Reitman

THE UNITED STATES MAIL ORDER INDUSTRY, by Maxwell Sroge

POWER DIRECT MARKETING, by "Rocket" Ray Jutkins

DIRECT MARKETING CHECKLISTS, by John Stockwell and Henry Shaw

STRATEGIC DATABASE MARKETING, by Rob Jackson and Paul Wang

SECRETS OF SUCCESSFUL DIRECT MAIL, by Richard V. Benson

SALES LETTERS THAT SIZZLE, by Herschell Gordon Lewis

SUCCESSFUL ADVERTISING RESEARCH METHODS, by Jack Haskins and Alice Kendrick

CASES IN ADVERTISING MANAGEMENT, edited by Terence Nevett

STRATEGIC ADVERTISING CAMPAIGNS, by Don E. Schultz and Beth E. Barnes

WHICH AD PULLED BEST?, by Philip Ward Burton and Scott C. Purvis

COPYCHASERS ON CREATING BUSINESS TO BUSINESS ADS, by Edmund O. Lawler

STRATEGY IN ADVERTISING, by Leo Bogart

HOW TO PRODUCE CREATIVE ADVERTISING, by Ann Keding and Thomas Bivins

HOW TO DEVELOP A SUCCESSFUL ADVERTISING PLAN, by James W. Taylor

ADVERTISING IN SOCIETY, by Roxanne Hovland and Gary Wilcox

ESSENTIALS OF ADVERTISING STRATEGY, by Don E. Schultz and Stanley I. Tannenbaum

CHOOSING AND WORKING WITH YOUR ADVERTISING AGENCY, by William A. Wielbacher

CHOOSING AND WORKING WITH YOUR PUBLIC RELATIONS FIRM, by Thomas L. Harris

THE ADVERTISING AGENCY BUSINESS, by Herbert S. Gardner, Jr.

BUSINESS TO BUSINESS ADVERTISING, by Charles H. Patti, Steven W. Hartley and Susan L. Kennedy

BUSINESS TO BUSINESS MARKETING COMMUNICATIONS, by Fred Messner

BUSINESS TO BUSINESS DIRECT MARKETING, by Robert Bly

THE PUBLICITY HANDBOOK, by David Yale

HANDBOOK FOR PUBLIC RELATIONS WRITING, by Thomas Bivins

POWER PUBLIC RELATIONS, by Leonard Saffir and Jack Tarrant

NTC'S DICTIONARY OF ADVERTISING, by Jack Wiechmann

THE ADVERTISING PORTFOLIO, by Ann Marie Barry

MARKETING CORPORATE IMAGE, by James R. Gregory with Jack G. Wiechmann

BUILDING YOUR ADVERTISING BUSINESS, by David M. Lockett

ADVERTISING & MARKETING CHECKLISTS, by Ron Kaatz

ADVERTISING COPYWRITING, by Philip Ward Burton

HOW TO SUCCEED IN ADVERTISING WHEN ALL YOU HAVE IS TALENT, by Lawrence Minsky and Emily Thornt Calvo

GREAT ADVERTISING CAMPAIGNS, by Nicholas Ind

HOW TO APPROACH AN ADVERTISING AGENCY AND WALK AWAY WITH THE JOB YOU WANT, by Barbara Ganim

For further information or a current catalog, write:
NTC Business Books
a division of *NTC Publishing Group*
4255 West Touhy Avenue
Lincolnwood, Illinois 60646–1975